Enjoy the read.
Kate Vitasek

# GETTING TO WE

# GETTING TO WE

# Negotiating Agreements for Highly Collaborative Relationships

*Jeanette Nyden, Kate Vitasek, and David Frydlinger*

palgrave
macmillan

First published in 2013 by
PALGRAVE MACMILLAN®
in the United States—a division of St. Martin's Press LLC,
175 Fifth Avenue, New York, NY 10010.

Where this book is distributed in the UK, Europe and the rest of the world,
this is by Palgrave Macmillan, a division of Macmillan Publishers Limited,
registered in England, company number 785998, of Houndmills,
Basingstoke, Hampshire RG21 6XS.

Palgrave Macmillan is the global academic imprint of the above companies
and has companies and representatives throughout the world.

Palgrave® and Macmillan® are registered trademarks in the United States,
the United Kingdom, Europe and other countries.

ISBN: 978–1–137–29718–1

Library of Congress Cataloging-in-Publication Data

Nyden, Jeanette.
    Getting to we : negotiating agreements for highly collaborative
relationships / Jeanette Nyden, Kate Vitasek, and David Frydlinger.
        pages cm
    Includes bibliographical references and index.
    ISBN 978–1–137–29718–1 (alk. paper)
    1. Negotiation in business. 2. Interpersonal relations. 3. Organizational
behavior. I. Vitasek, Kate. II. Frydlinger, David. III. Title.

HD58.6.N93 2013
658.4′052—dc23                                                    2013003785

A catalogue record of the book is available from the British Library.

Design by Newgen Imaging Systems (P) Ltd., Chennai, India.

First edition: August 2013

10 9 8 7 6 5 4 3 2 1

# DEDICATION

*We would like to dedicate this book to our partners, who selflessly give us their time, support, and encouragement. Together, we live the principles embodied by* Getting to We *each day.*

*Tim, Greg, and Caroline: we are in your debt and appreciate all you have done for us.*

*Tim Lohraff (husband) and Isabella and Elizabeth Lohraff*
*Jeanette Nyden*

*Greg Picinich (husband) and Austin Picinich*
*Kate Vitasek*

*Caroline Frydlinger (wife) and Rebecka, Oskar and Klara*
*David Frydlinger*

# CONTENTS

# FIGURES

# INTRODUCTION

I n 2009 Kate Vitasek and Dr. Alex Miller, then associate dean of
the University of Tennessee's Center for Executive Education, got
together over a beer. They wanted to unwind and discuss the findings of a recent research project conducted by the university, which
had been funded by the United States Air Force. Vitasek was the lead
researcher.

The casual discussion between colleagues turned out to be a pro-
phetic conversation; you will realize why in a moment.

Vitasek and her fellow researchers were studying highly successful
performance-based, collaborative business relationships. They wanted
to know what made those relationships successful. The key finding was
that the parties involved had created symbiotic relationships where
"win-win" was not a glib marketing term. Rather, win-win thinking was
deeply embedded in the parties' relationship. It influenced how they
worked together with shared goals to drive innovation and create value
that did not exist before.

The research was codified into five rules and their emergent
methodology was called Vested. If followed, Vested had the power to
help all companies design their own hyper-collaborative win-win relationships, just like the companies studied in the research. The team
realized early on that the methodology had the transformative potential of Lean and Six Sigma, other well-known business management
philosophies.

That evening, Vitasek and Dr. Miller lamented the reality that the
business world does not typically adopt or embrace academic research.
Instead, great research often remains trapped inside university walls
and bureaucracy.

They wondered, "Just how could the researchers get the business
world to adopt their emergent methodology and business model?"

Vitasek and Miller had an epiphany. They already knew the answer before they asked the question.

The answer was in their own research: take the emerging Vested business model and apply the rules and principles to create their own highly collaborative Vested relationships with thought leaders and experts from the academic and business world. These experts could help them take the Vested concept and institutionalize it across all businesses, in all industries, all across the world.

That meeting was in 2009. The potential Vitasek and Miller glimpsed that night is a reality.

The work behind this book is the product of one of those Vested collaborations.

## THE EVOLUTION OF GETTING TO WE

Vitasek shared the Vested mindset and an advance copy of the first Vested book, *Vested Outsourcing: Five Rules That Will Transform Outsourcing*, with Jeanette Nyden.

Vitasek had known Nyden for several years and considered her a trusted friend. A lawyer by trade, Nyden had created a successful negotiation training company. She agreed to provide feedback to Vitasek about the book.

Nyden read the book and immediately saw a tremendous opportunity that also had the potential to solve a systemic flaw in how companies negotiated. To make the Vested mindset and the methodology truly transformative, business people would have to adopt a different way of negotiating. The atmosphere of gamesmanship present in most commercial negotiations needed replacement, but with what?

As a young trial attorney, Nyden saw firsthand the impact of good intentions gone wrong. She had grown weary and frustrated watching clients spend hundreds of thousands of dollars and countless hours fighting over what was "fair." She transitioned her practice and began helping companies negotiate fair and balanced deals that would *not* end up in court.

Nyden realized that a complete paradigm shift was needed in negotiation. From teaching strategies and tactics for negotiating a specific deal to the specifics of how to create a powerful relationship that could withstand the pressures of a dynamic business environment, everything needed to be transformed.

Through this transformation, the Getting to We negotiation process was born.

The Getting to We process changes the goal of the negotiation from the deal itself to the relationship. Following the Getting to We negotiation process helps companies change how they view the relationship—helping them embrace Vested's what's-in-it-for-we (WIIFWe) mindset. The WIIFWe mindset is the foundation of a Vested relationship; it is a change in social norms from a what's-in-it-for-me (WIIFMe) mindset. WIIFWe is *the* philosophical mantra forming the architecture for a collaborative and trusting relationship. Once embraced, a WIIFWe mindset has the power to deliver a competitive advantage for the parties long after the deal is signed.

David Frydlinger, a Swedish attorney and partner at Lindahl Law Firm, joined Nyden and Vitasek in the creation of the Getting to We process. Frydlinger—a Vested Certified Deal Architect—is well-schooled in the Vested methodology. He also witnessed the inherent conflict between using conventional negotiation processes and tactics as companies set out to adopt the Vested mindset and business model. Frydlinger also wrote a book in Swedish about the power of using social norms in business negotiations, and saw the power of codifying the power of the Getting to We negotiation process.

The Getting to We negotiation process has become instrumental in helping companies achieve success as they pursue Vested relationships. Through the exploration of Vested, companies found they could use the Getting to We process to help them regardless of whether they were able to follow all five of Vested's rules for creating a highly collaborative business model. The team also found that companies could use the process to improve internal relationships.

What Miller and Vitasek envisioned over a beer that night has become reality. Today Nyden and Fyrdlinger are two among dozens of organizations and individuals that are an integral part of an ecosystem of researchers, thought leaders, and business visionaries focused on building upon—as well as on rolling out—the Vested mindset, methodology, and business model to organizations all over the world. Their relationship—like the many others—has become Vested *because* it is built with the rules and principles of the research that set it all in motion.

## OVERVIEW OF THE STRUCTURE OF THIS BOOK

This book is about the Getting to We process: a how-to guide that creates a paradigm shift in how people and organizations approach negotiations. Getting to We shares a detailed—yet simple to follow—five-step process any company can adopt when it negotiates a deal. The process goes well beyond helping companies negotiate the specifics of a deal; it helps them create a solid foundation for the overall relationship itself. This process helps businesses change their mindset, which in turn builds understanding, comfort, and trust so they are able to work together effectively in a sustainable relationship. This sustainability has the power to deliver a competitive advantage for the parties, not just the party with the most power or the one with the better negotiating skills.

Section I helps parties prepare for the Getting to We process by establishing a solid foundation of trust, transparency, and compatibility. This is the first step in the process. This section also shows how to close any gaps companies on the Getting to We path might have regarding trust, transparency, and compatibility. Successful partnerships first lay the foundation for a strong relationship that embraces a WIIFWe approach.

Section II explores steps two and three of the five steps in the Getting to We process. This section includes creating a shared vision and agreeing upon a common set of guiding principles for the relationship. These steps in the process cannot be ignored. Skipping these steps could pose problems later in the Getting to We process as the vision and principles play a dominant role in every aspect of the relationship and provide much-needed focus to drive collaborative behaviors.

Section III covers the fourth step in the Getting to We process—Negotiating as We. Negotiating as We means three things. First, the parties agree to follow four collaborative negotiation rules. These rules are not the same rules parties use to negotiate conventional agreements. Second, it means consciously using collaborative negotiation strategies and tactics. The old school tactics many business people learned are not applicable to negotiating highly collaborative relationships. Finally, the parties will create and allocate value for long-term mutual success. This

Creative Value Allocation process replaces competitive tensions nego-tiators often feel when negotiating money with a process that is more collaborative.

Last, section IV explores the final step in the Getting to We process—Living as We. At this point in the Getting to We process, most negotia-tors think they are done because organizations have transformed the relationship into a true partnership. But of course they are not done. Each party must live We. This section provides valuable insight into *liv-ing* a WIIFWe mindset and offers techniques to develop a relationship management structure that supports that mindset. This section also profiles companies that have embraced the WIIFWe mindset and nego-tiated the very nature of their relationship. Their success is real.

## A NOTE ON TERMINOLOGY

Before jumping into the Getting to We negotiating process, it is impor-tant to understand some of the key words and terminology used in this book.

**WIIFWe mindset**—What's-in-in-for-we (WIIFWe) is *the* philosophi-cal mantra for all highly collaborative relationships. It is also the foun-dation for a Vested relationship. WIIFWe stands in stark opposition to the more conventional what's-in-it-for-me (WIIFMe) mindset commonly found in many business relationships, which pits people and companies against one another, each trying to get the best possible deal. By con-trast, WIIFWe embodies a framework for a collaborative and trusting relationship.

**We**—"We" is an abbreviation for WIIFWe. The abbreviation should not be confused with the common meaning of the word "we."

**Getting to We**—Getting to We is a new negotiation paradigm. It combines the WIIFWe mindset with a five-step process for negotiat-ing highly collaborative relationships. The heart of Getting to We is an agreement to abide by six fundamental social norms that form the guid-ing principles for the entire relationship. Therefore, companies that want to develop highly collaborative relationships, whether with current or new partners, must embrace the principles and follow the process.

**Vested**—WIIFWe is the mindset of Vested®. Vested is a methodol-ogy and business model for highly-collaborative, win-win relationships. Vested combines outcome-based, shared-value and relational economics principles. This enables the parties to "expand and share the pie" with a focus on creating value for each party that did not exist previously. Getting to We is one precondition to developing a Vested relationship.

The words **partner, partners,** and **partnership** are used interchangeably with **party, parties,** and **relationship** throughout this book. Companies that follow the Getting to We process are not creating a legal partnership. Rather they are developing a highly collaborative relationship in which the parties may choose to interact with each other as non-legal partners in each other's success.

CHAPTER 1

# WHAT ARE YOU G-E-T-T-I-N-G TO?

For more than thirty years, businesses have been indoctrinated with the idea that the prize in negotiation is to get the deal. The deal is the focus. Hundreds of books have been written to teach negotiation, from *Getting to Yes*, *Geting Past No*, *Getting More* to even the virtues of *Start with No*. The focus of these works is transactional in nature and has readers concentrating on the strategies and tactics for negotiating the deal. Negotiation is about "this deal," "this time," and under "this set of business and legal terms." Negotiators think, "Get a signature, and you are done." It is a done deal, and the deal is the deal.

Here lies the systemic problem: Transactions are quick, short-term exchanges. The deals they create are static, but of course a business environment is not. And static deals often lose equilibrium, where the deal is no longer perceived as fair by one or both parties. Business headlines are littered with stories of good deals gone bad. Law firms bill hundreds of millions of dollars in fees each year as companies battle over what went wrong, who is to blame, and how to balance out the losses when the deal was the focus in the negotiation. At a minimum, the individuals involved have increased frustration and companies are burdened with increased transaction costs. When this happens parties find themselves back again at the negotiating table under new circumstances. What a waste of precious time and money better spent on creating innovation and growth for the parities.

What if negotiations for a business relationship were viewed through a different lens? A lens where the purpose of the negotiation is to lay down the crucial foundational elements of the relationship itself, rather than negotiate the specific scope and terms and conditions for the transaction at hand?

Think about that. The relationship as the focus of the deal. The specifics of how the parties will manage the relationship become the vade mecum (in essence the basic guidebook) for the relationship outlining how the business parties can work together successfully in a dynamic business environment of constant change, increasing risk, and uncharted opportunities.

Does that make sense? Or more appropriately: why wouldn't it make sense?

Most organizations have at least a handful of highly strategic business relationships or partnerships that have a direct impact on a company's bottom line; even more important, they have a direct impact on customer satisfaction and therefore on market share. And these highly strategic relationships typically involve much more than a one and done transaction. Some good examples are:

- supply chain service providers who manage the day-to-day distribution of products directly to a company's customers
- customer service and technical support providers who act on a company's behalf to take customer orders or answer customer complaints or solve problems
- information technology partners who provide the critical IT backbone to make a company run
- business process outsourcing firms that perform key internal functions, such as finance operations/accounting or human resources support
- facilities and real estate management service providers who are deeply embedded in the day-to-day running of the physical assets of the business

In the cases above, there can easily be hundreds or even thousands of transactions each day. The classic approach is to negotiate a rigid scope of work and price—to ensure that the deal in question is "fair."

The problem is that business is highly dynamic and in the midst of a massive digital and social transformation. The new normal is that there is no "normal" and constant change is the status quo. A fair negotiation today is likely to not be fair tomorrow when circumstances change—and they will. Business assumptions will likely not remain static: volumes change, work mix changes, uncontrollable costs can have erratic swings impacting profitability. The switching costs to change service providers are very high, often costing companies tens to hundreds of thousands of dollars. And the costs of operational risk and nonperformance can be staggering or can even lead to a reputation risk that could cause the downfall of the company.

*Getting to We* is a book about negotiating. It is not, however, a typical negotiation book when compared to the hundreds of current books on this topic. Existing negotiation books focus on explaining best practices on how to get a deal or how to get a better deal. *Getting to We* is a book that opens the way to developing a new mindset and process for negotiating business relationships where the success of the relationship actually matters. *Getting to We* teaches:

- Why negotiating the very nature of the relationship is as important as negotiating the specifics of the deal.
- How to establish a common set of principles or relationship norms that drive and support collaboration.
- The rules, strategies, and tactics for negotiating highly collaborative relationships.
- How to create long-term mutually beneficial value for all parties by allocating risks and rewards in a fair and balanced manner.
- How following the common principles as the relationship strives to achieve its vision is critical for continued success.

Getting to We is the negotiation process and strategy for Vested relationships. As covered in the introduction, Vested is a mindset, methodology, business model, and movement for highly collaborative relationships that create mutual value through innovation. Vested is based on award-winning research conducted by the University of Tennessee.[1]

Getting to We embraces the philosophical mantra what's-in-it-for-we (WIIFWe) and includes a simple process for creating the social norms of a Vested relationship. With both the mindset and the process, companies develop highly collaborative and sustainable business relationships. The process of Getting to We forms the architecture for a collaborative and trusting endeavor. Business giants like Procter & Gamble, Jones

Lang LaSalle, McDonald's, Microsoft, Accenture, Dell, GENCO ATC, and the joint venture Kaiser-Hill have embraced a Vested WIIFWe approach, and the long-term results are astounding. By negotiating the relationship, these companies achieved new levels of opportunity and innovation, uncontested market share, efficiency, and untethered problem solving—for them and the companies they work with. It started with a WIIFWe mindset.

As Vested is adopted by global companies and organizations, we have codified how to achieve the goal of negotiating relationships. Learning to work together not just in the present, but also planning for the future, parties build understanding, comfort, and trust. Sufficient understanding enables each to prosper, regardless of the inevitable changes ahead. In Vested, negotiators and leaders are taught that the secret to a good deal is not getting to a deal or even getting the best deal at a particular point in time, but negotiating the foundational principles of a relationship that can sustainably deliver a competitive advantage for all the parties long after the deal is signed.

Whether or not an agreement or partnership evolves from the Vested WIIFWe mindset to Vested's business model for highly collaborative relationships, negotiating relationships to create the mindset of WIIFWe has the power to deliver a competitive advantage for the parties long after the deal is signed.

Ongoing strategic business relationships should strongly consider embracing a WIIFWe mindset and following the Getting to We process outlined in this book.

## IS GETTING TO WE *REALLY* DIFFERENT?

The difference between negotiating a deal and a relationship starts with the goal of the negotiation and continues with the process and tactics that are used during the negotiation. Learning to negotiate the essential nature of the relationship is about getting to the mindset of long-term success for the benefit of the partnership and each partner.

Let's first examine the classic negotiating mentality. At a recent procurement trade conference a commercial contracting employee from a Fortune 100 company was sharing his version of negotiation and contracting best practices. The company representative told the packed room, "My job is to make sure that my deals are profitable for my company and my company alone."[2] This WIIFMe mindset fuels modern negotiation strategy and tactics. In fact, it is so ingrained in today's business culture that many organizations may even tie bonuses to how much a buying company can save or a service provider can gain in a negotiation.

What has led to this mindset? One could argue that it is the nature of capitalism itself dating back to Adam Smith's "invisible hand" theory of economics. Smith published his theories in 1776 in *The Wealth of Nations*.[3] The underlying assumptions, which are still prevalent today, are that when each business strives for its own interest, even at the expense of its partner's interests, the resulting agreement must be fair. The logic is that in a free market society, companies have the choice to enter into agreements, and therefore they would not agree to something that works against their self-interest. Thus, each business's striving for its self-interest balances the interests of the others.

While negotiation tactics and contract law have evolved over time, the basic approach has stayed pretty much the same over the years: People enter contracts at arm's length to pursue material ends, and risks are negotiated and assigned at the time of the contract. While either party has the ability to walk away from a business deal, the party with the most power or negotiating skills usually gets the better deal.

Getting to We is different. It is not focused on getting the best deal today—or even on getting a deal at all. It is a philosophical mantra and process for creating a strong foundation where parties can fluidly adjust to business needs and risks as they arise and do so in a harmonious and productive manner. The premise is that by agreeing to the foundational nature of the relationship itself, the organizations can get to a fair and balanced deal not only for the present, but for any circumstances in the future as well. Getting to We is about negotiating the guiding principles of the relationship first and then and only then negotiating the specific aspects of the transaction(s).

## CULTURAL NORMS GUIDE

One might ask, "Why should I care about the sustainability of a business relationship. It's about the profitability of the deal, isn't it?" That is a question that academics from all walks of life around the world ask themselves as well.

Ronald Dworkin, a professor of philosophy and law who wrote extensively about ethics, morality, equality, justice, and the unity of value, was renowned for his research into the importance of establishing social norms in relationships. Much of his work emphasizes the role social norms play in regulating society and producing fair outcomes. By connecting economic and political theory, Dworkin offered fresh insights on how to effectively develop a partnership environment.

Dworkin argued the (often unwritten and unspoken) principles partners choose have the power to change the very essence of how they work together. Specifically, the principles (or social norms) have the power to drive behaviors and thus have a cause and effect that can dictate certain outcomes. For example, if partners choose to follow principles that are fair, outcomes will also be fair. If they choose to be short-sighted and opportunistic, the nature of their relationship will be short-sighted and opportunistic.

One of the most fascinating research projects on opportunism and collaboration comes from Robert Axelrod. Axelrod, a professor of political science and public policy, wanted to understand the power of cooperation. He invited game theorists to compete in a computerized tournament to see who could devise a strategy to win in a classic game known as the Prisoner's Dilemma.[4]

The game shows why two individuals might not cooperate even if it appears that it is in their best interests to do so.[5] All purely rational self-interested prisoners would remain silent, but instead what often happens is that each prisoner betrays the other prisoner ("defects") by implicating the other prisoner in the crime, resulting in stiff sentences for each of them. The irony of the Prisoner's Dilemma game is that both prisoners actually get the best outcome if they both remain silent ("cooperate").

To cooperate or not to cooperate? This is a simple yet profound question.

Axelrod invited game theorists to play the Prisoner's Dilemma game over four rounds with each player having four opportunities to either cooperate or defect. His findings were seminal: The greatest odds of winning came from a strategy known as "tit-for-tat." A tit-for-tat strategy can best be defined by having a player echo (reciprocate) what the other player did in the previous move. For example, if person A cooperates, person B will cooperate. If person A suddenly defects, then person B should follow suit and also defect. A defection is a competitive move that is characterized as noncooperative and self-serving in nature.

Axelrod's findings were described in his book *The Evolution of Cooperation*.[6] Playing "nice"—or cooperating—led to the best results and maximized mutual gain for both players. Axelrod summarized his findings as follows:[7]

- Be nice: cooperate, never be the first to defect. The best results come when both parties consistently cooperate.
- Be provocable: return defection for defection, cooperation for cooperation.
- Don't be envious: be fair with your partner. This means resisting the urge to optimize your position at the expense of your partner's position.
- Don't be too clever: don't try to be tricky in the pursuit of trying to game the system for your benefit.

After reading Axelrod's summary, it's worth asking why negotiators fall prey to trying to outwit their counterparts at the negotiating table by using deceptive negotiation practices aimed at winning at the other party's expense. The answer is simple. First, as soon as one partner defects the other person will automatically defect. Second, many of the players who negotiate on behalf of their companies have an inherent incentive to simply get the deal done and to get the best deal for their companies. The larger the deal and the more that is at stake, the more prone companies are to bring in professional negotiators, procurement professionals, and/or lawyers to ensure the company is getting a good deal. This is especially true when the object is to get to a deal this time and when the relationship is short-term. Many companies ask themselves why they should bother to cooperate in the last round if they can win more by making one more demand or concession (defecting)?

In such a business culture people justify opportunism. Opportunism can be defined as the desire and the ability to take advantage of a partner—or anyone!—at a given time simply because one can. Unfortunately, many companies don't view opportunism as a bad thing. Rather, opportunism is business as usual. Businesses have developed norms for their business relationships that encourage or protect against opportunism.

An internationally renowned outsourcing attorney said, "Think about the last time that a service provider went out of its way for its customer and then the first time that service provider doesn't meet one service level agreement. The customer slams the service provider with a financial penalty. It's a bad economic decision. That decision to seek a penalty will drive the service provider's behavior to do just enough for compliance with the contract and nothing more."[8] In other words, the customer acts opportunistically when it disregards the service provider's good behavior and focuses its attention on the poor performance by seeking a financial penalty. Since the service provider was not rewarded in any away for its additional efforts it will not likely go out of its way to exceed service levels in the future.

Opportunism can take many forms—and can even occur well *after* a deal is negotiated. For example, a global retailer sends out a letter to suppliers requesting that they provide a rebate to offset the global retailer's losses in other areas. Or a service provider intentionally bids very low to win the business only to recoup the losses later by claiming many costly change orders. Maybe a company's procurement group pressures its suppliers to offer another 5 percent in savings at the midpoint of the life of the agreement.

To put Axelrod's tit-for-tat concepts next to Dworkin's concepts about social norms driving behaviors, *modern businesses have created "negotiation norms" that foster destructive behaviors and actually destroy value rather than promoting value creation through mutual self-interest.*

Despite the very real potential that the relationship can be permanently damaged, businesses often encourage opportunistic behaviors, both at the bargaining table and after the contract is signed. Thus, many negotiators ask how to break the cycle.

## ENCOURAGING COOPERATION

The original research on the hyper-collaborative Vested relationship model is based on the fact that collaborative relationships don't necessarily end after a short time. Rather, partners continue to work together. Those most successful are those that choose a collaborative path.[9] Encouraging cooperation is critical in an atmosphere that supports opportunism. There are two factors that influence cooperative behavior.

First, Axelrod describes what he calls "the shadow of the future,"[10] which embodies the likelihood that the parties will meet again. If the shadow of the future looms large enough—players believe that they will meet again—they are more likely to cooperate since there is no path out of the dilemma by successive rounds of competitive behavior.

In long-term collaborative relationships the future starts to influence the present. In We partnerships the shadow of the future is large enough to warrant successive rounds of cooperative behavior.

Second, Axelrod points to "additional activities." Additional activities have the power to change how the parties behave in the game. One significant additional activity that changes the Prisoner's Dilemma game is staying in the game. If neither party can leave or "eliminate" the other, players tend to choose a different set of actions.

Axelrod's tit-for-tat game lasted only four rounds and the game was over. Both prisoners knew when the game would end. Similarly, businesses in short-term business relationships *think* they know when the relationship will end. Despite some short-term contracts, relationships between parties can actually go on for many years, one or two years at a time.

A leading bank realized the importance of Axelrod's two lessons regarding the shadow of the future and additional activity. The bank was renegotiating a contract with an outsourced service provider. Over the course of many months, the bank's team was cooperative. But at the eleventh hour, the bank demanded a 10 percent across-the-board reduction in the rate it paid the service provider's employees. The bank demonstrated classic negotiation tactics. The bank thought it could defect by demanding a price reduction.

The eleventh hour demand was a quintessential case of opportunism. When one organization is solely focused on getting to an agreement without regard for the long-term effects on the relationship, the organization can justify opportunistic behavior.

When the service provider called the bank's bluff and suggested it would rather leave the relationship than take a price cut—the ultimate defection—the bank retreated. The bank failed to realize that it and the service provider were both in a relationship. The bank did not want the service provider to exit; it just wanted more money. The bank thought the service provider would cooperate and provide some sort of price cut.

When the service provider threatened to defect, the bank had to make a different decision: it would have to choose a cooperative move to keep the service provider in the relationship.

The good news is that the organizations realized they were in their own version of the Prisoner's Dilemma. Continuing down that path— regardless of the specifics of the new deal—would create stress on the relationship and could eventually send the relationship into a death spiral by turning a good relationship into a poor relationship. Instead, the companies paused the negotiations and began their journey to We.

The example poses a very important question: how do parties keep the cycle of cooperative moves when an opportunity presents itself to grab some short-term gains? A pure tit-for-tat as a strategy will not automatically lead to successive rounds of cooperative behavior because each player has the choice to defect.

## GETTING BEYOND YES

Too often business people approach a negotiation by looking through a lens of self-interest, which defeats the purpose of looking for mutual gains. In their best-selling negotiating book *Getting to Yes*,[11] Fisher and Ury tell the classic tale of how to divide an orange. Their story illustrates the conventional philosophy regarding mutual gain. In the orange story, two people negotiate to divide one orange. Positional bargaining would split the orange in some fashion—in half or perhaps with the party with the most power getting two-thirds and the weaker party getting one-third.

Fisher and Ury presented a new paradigm known as interest-based bargaining in 1981. Interest-based bargaining allows each person to share their interests with the hope of finding a mutual gain. For example, one party may want the pulp while the other party may want the peel. Fisher and Ury taught that interest-based bargaining allows the parties to seek creativity in their negotiations to achieve their interests. Thus, in the Fisher and Ury analogy, the parties' self-interests are maximized, with each person getting exactly what is wanted: one would get all of the peel and the other all of the pulp.

The problem is that Fisher and Ury's approach falls short of achieving real mutual gain. In this example, people are still fighting over one orange today. This short-term and opportunistic mindset is myopic and inefficient. But companies still do it.

Ultimately, as negotiators embrace the WIIFWe mindset, partners begin to view the relationship as a unique and individual entity with interests of its own. Changing the lens to view the partnership as its own entity with its own interests in addition to each partner's interests solves the problem of fighting over one orange today. Using a WIIFWe mindset changes the question from what is in *my* self-interest to what move will generate value for the partnership. The parties would then find solutions to work together to perhaps plant an orange tree allowing *both* to prosper from an increased harvest. Planting that tree requires a paradigm shift.

## BREAK THE OPPORTUNISTIC CYCLE

Many see the WIIFWe mindset as a paradigm shift. Getting to We starts with making the choice to break the cycle of opportunism by adopting a mindset that cooperation is the right approach. While Axelrod's findings were based on a computerized model, humans have the power to choose their behaviors and cooperate. Breaking the cycle of opportunism means teaching people that making a competitive move triggers a competitive countermove. It is in everyone's best interest to avoid opportunism in long-term business relationships where the parties have chosen to work together.

Unfortunately, breaking the cycle of opportunism is not easy. A psychological bias, called partisan perceptions, distorts the impact of a competitive move. Partisan perceptions skew judgment of our actions and our partners' actions. For example, if someone tells a lie, she tells herself self-serving justifications for her actions, but if her partner tells a lie, she evaluates the behavior (telling the lie) critically and as being far worse than the lie she told.

Partisan perceptions, coupled with a series of competitive behaviors, create downward pressures in the relationship. The "defection" becomes ever-worsening behavior, justifiable in the eyes of the doer and unjustifiable in the eyes of the recipient. Many business relationships live in various stages of this death spiral. This process starts with one person justifying a purely self-serving, non-cooperative action.

Negotiating the true nature of the relationship at the outset means that the parties move out of the competitive tit-for-tat cycle of actions and instead go on to create a negotiation atmosphere for encouraging cooperation.

Three things about a WIIFWe relationship alter the conventional tit-for-tat strategy, and especially defecting in the final round of negotiations. First, the players turn into partners for success. They set out to enter into a long-term relationship where each partner intends not to "eliminate" their partner by moving to another supplier or customer. The intent transforms a transactional business relationship into a strategic relationship.

Second, the relationship adheres to a common set of principles that drive cooperative behavior. Finally, We partnerships live We in daily interactions and use a formal, documented governance structure to ensure compliance with cooperative behavior. Thus the relationship generates successive rounds of cooperative tit-for-tat thinking to create value that is mutually beneficial to both partners.

## GETTING TO WE

Getting to We is a process. Once companies have chosen to embrace a WIIFWe mindset, they are ready to walk the path of actually Getting to We. Companies and organizations wanting the tangible and intangible benefits of hyper-collaboration—whether with internal partners or external partners—will need to follow a five-step path. Approaching the partnership formation from the wrong mindset *and* negotiating things in the wrong sequence can destroy any chance of negotiating a long-term mutually beneficial relationship.

The Getting to We process comprises five distinct steps: the first four take the parties to We, and the fifth step ensures that the parties live We. None of the steps should be skipped. Cutting corners will only derail efforts at Getting to We. The five steps are outlined briefly here. Each step is discussed in greater detail throughout the rest of this book.

**Step 1: Getting ready for WIIFWe.** This initial step looks at three foundational elements for a successful collaborative relationship: trust, transparency, and compatibility. At the completion of this step the parties know whether they have a solid enough foundation to move to the next step. If they don't, they work on solidifying their relationship. If they have a good foundation, they move on to step two. Completing this first step enables partners to determine whether a WIIFWe mindset has merit and whether they are willing to explore establishing or renegotiating a highly collaborative relationship.

**Step 2: Jointly agree on a shared vision for the partnership.** Each party will enter the discussion with its own vision, which is perfectly valid, of course. But the parties transform those separate visions into a shared vision. The shared vision gives the partnership its purpose beyond a series of transactions. Furthermore, it will guide the partners, not only throughout the negotiation process, but throughout the entire term of the relationship. Aiming for the same target sets the stage for the third step in the path to We.

**Step 3: Collaboratively negotiate the guiding principles** *for the partnership.* The Getting to We process *demands* that partners not only improve the relationship but also abide by a set of principles to drive highly collaborative behavior. This is the critical step that distinguishes highly collaborative relationships from average functioning relationships. The principles provide the mindset to support the partners on their journey to live We. Without guiding principles to prevent opportunism and competitive tit-for-tat moves partners will not behave in a collaborative manner with each other.

**Step 4: Negotiate as We—it is now time to begin to negotiate the deal.** Partners following the Getting to We process *must not start* by negotiating the detailed specifics of the deal such as the scope of work, pricing, and terms and conditions. Rather, they must first establish the mechanisms they will jointly use as they negotiate the specifics. This includes agreeing on the "negotiation rules," the strategies and tactics, and the approach for ensuring the deal specifics are fair and balanced, especially when it comes to how the parties deal with risk allocation and creating value. Once the partners have agreed to these mechanisms, they will use them to gain consensus on the specifics of their agreement.

**Step 5: Living as We.** Now the partners have reached the final step on their journey, living as We. Living as We occurs when the partners maintain a focus on the shared vision and guiding principles throughout the duration of the relationship. Because relationships are dynamic, the partners choose to focus on relationship management by taking actions and measures required to keep the relationship highly collaborative. The principles continue to play a critical role by driving the partners' daily behaviors.

The Getting to We process coupled with the WIIFWe mindset enables the parties to negotiate the relationship itself and set that relationship on a course for continuous collaboration.

## ARE YOU READY TO START YOUR JOURNEY TO WE?

Does it ever seem that your business relationships feel like a tug-of-war, with people tugging back and forth every time there is the slightest change? You might be suffering from a negative tit-for-tat dynamic in your relationship. As you were reading this chapter, did you pause and think of instances when you or your business partners may have justified making a competitive move? Or ponder how you retaliated when a partner made a competitive move?

If you did, you likely have a personal ethos or mindset that can support a WIIFWe mindset. But believing in a WIIFWe mindset is much easier than getting an organization and a business partner's organization to adopt the philosophical mantra. For this reason, we offer this book as a resource guide to help you on your journey.

The transformation from a WIIFMe mindset to a WIIFWe mindset begins when companies and organizations negotiate the *very nature* of their relationship, rather than a series of transactions aimed at exchanging goods and services. As you challenge your thinking and determine whether WIIFWe is right for you, remember that it is impossible to get to the WIIFWe mindset by having one or even 100 back-and-forth conversations aimed at reaching an agreement one transaction at time. Instead, focus attention on developing a stable and flexible relationship and only then turn to transactions—the exchange of goods and services.

Those who adopt the mindset and lay the foundation for relationship success will improve their chances of achieving success far greater than they can imagine. Companies that get to We set the stage to transform their business as usual relationship into a powerful partnership capable of generating long-term economic value for themselves and for the partnership. Some of our favorite success stories are examined in *Vested: How P&G, McDonald's and Microsoft are Redefining Winning in Business Relationships,*[12] which profiles some of the world's best business relationships. Unlike *Vested,* this book does not go into the success stories of the relationships. Instead, it focuses on how these companies, as well as many others, laid the groundwork for success by challenging the WIIFMe mindset and by choosing to adopt a WIIFWe mindset. *Getting to We* also profiles the journey and struggles for companies that are just starting to adopt a WIIFWe philosophical mantra.

At this point, it's helpful to collect your thoughts before moving on to the first step in the process of Getting to We. The following questions will help you decide how to best move forward in your organization's journey to the WIIFWe mentality.

---

**Are You Ready?**

- How comfortable are you (or is your organization) with the WIIFWe mindset?
- Are you or is your organization willing to consider negotiating the very nature of a partnership first before negotiating the transactions that flow from the relationship?
- Are you or is your organization willing to move from seeking short-term transaction-based benefits to long-term benefits that mutually benefit the partnership and each partner in the right kind of opportunity?
- Are you willing to be a champion for the WIIFWe philosophy and the process both internally and with the right partner?

---

People drive business. People drive innovation. People have to deal with changes. It's time to evolve negotiation practices where the relationship is the substance, not the specifics of a transaction. Unleash the power of a WIIFWe mindset in your organization.

# STEP 1: ESTABLISH A FOUNDATION OF TRUST, TRANSPARENCY, AND COMPATIBILITY

Most relationships are not perfect at first. But to get to a WIIFWe mindset, partners must have some measure of trust, transparency, and compatibility. These three components are the building blocks of a solid and stable foundation.

*Trust* is *the* core quality of any collaborative partnership. Trust is the enabler for everything else that follows on the path to We. Trust lowers transaction costs, fosters innovation, and provides the necessary space for the flexibility and agility needed in today's markets.

Trust requires a high degree of *transparency* between the parties, providing them with the information needed to perform to the mutual benefit of all. Without trust, parties are less likely to share information openly. Without transparency, it is difficult for partners to agree to follow the guiding principles, to negotiate a financially beneficial win-win, and to continue to embody the We philosophy.

Finally, a collaborative relationship is helped along by a certain level of *compatibility* between the parties. Compatibility is made up of two elements, behaviors and culture. Compatibility fosters an atmosphere of trust because the partners' behaviors and culture are somewhat aligned. Compatibility and trust make possible the openness necessary to solve problems.

This section describes how to close gaps in trust, transparency, and compatibility. Those who are successful will lay the foundation for a strong relationship that can embrace a WIIFWe mindset.

Chapter 2 shows that trust is the cornerstone enabling parties to embrace the WIIFWe mindset and follow the Getting to We process. Without sufficient trust, the parties will have a difficult—if not impossible time—of getting to We.

Chapter 3 discusses the bond that transparency and compatibility have in building a strong foundation for the relationship. Awareness plays a critical role in understanding the level of compatibility parties share. This chapter also offers the reader a tool to assess compatibility and trust.

# CHAPTER 2

# TRUST

Trust is the essential starting point for all We partnerships. Intuitively, everyone understands the importance of trust in commercial relationships. The Nobel laureate economist Kenneth Arrow agrees: "Virtually every commercial transaction has within itself an element of trust, certainly any transaction conducted over a period of time."[1] Without a fair degree of trust, companies simply will not continue on the journey to We. A lack of trust sets a hurdle that is too high to jump.

Trust exists when a person or organization has confidence in a positive result even when the issues and outcomes are out of its control, and there is risk of a potentially negative consequence. Partners also trust one another when neither side has reason to expect that it will be taken advantage of, and whenever possible it will even do things that advance the other's interests.

## ECONOMIC BENEFITS OF TRUST

Research from the International Association for Contract and Commercial Management (IACCM) suggests companies are not very trusting. Its research reveals most contracts remain dominated by self-interested, protectionist terms rather than provisions that promote collaboration between trading partners. A key finding is that companies spend the most amount of time negotiating limitations of liability and shifting risk, a telling indication that companies simply don't trust their partners.[2]

Trust establishes the conditions for *productive collaboration*. Companies with high degrees of trust can spend their energy leveraging each other's core strengths and creating value. Adam Smith wrote in *Wealth of*

*Nations*[3] that the "division of labor" was the number one factor behind growth and progress in society. Two individuals working on a project will be more productive if they split the work, letting each do what that person does best—that is, if they cooperate. This applies equally to the nail factory Smith wrote about and to other commercial and noncommercial relationships. It is, however, important to understand that Smith's observation about cooperation in the form of division of labor requires trust—trust that the other person will actually do what he says he'll do.

Trust enables collaboration in two ways. First, a trusting relationship unleashes the extraordinary power of human innovation and creativity. As levels of trust increase, parties are relieved of the burden of having to look constantly over their shoulders. Once partners are less cautious, they can spend their time and energy in the pursuit of more creative solutions. Thus, trust allows companies to invest in the future because they trust that their counterpart will continue to support their strategic objectives.

Second, trust decreases transaction costs. Transaction costs entail the costs associated with using the "market" to produce something for your company and can come in the form of deciding where to buy a good or service instead of making or performing the service yourself. Trust makes sure the benefits of cooperation exceed the benefits of going to the market to get a better deal. By lowering transaction costs, companies are free to use their energies to pursue cooperative potential.

Studies show the importance of trust for economic growth and that its absence adds to the cost of doing business.[4] Think back to a recent interaction with an untrustworthy person. A certain amount of what is done before, during, and after that interaction is likely directed at ensuring that there is no deception by the other person. This activity is wasteful, as it does not directly create value for anyone. This is a transaction cost. Often the transaction costs are so high that they exceed the benefits of doing business together.

Stephen M.R. Covey's book *Speed of Trust* outlines seven "organizational taxes" that are directly related to low trust. These are all examples of increased transaction costs due to low trust.[5]

1. **Redundancy** is unnecessary duplication. It stems from the mindset that people cannot be trusted unless they are being closely watched.

2. **Bureaucracy** is when too many rules and regulations are in place, when too many people have to "sign off" on something.

3. **Politics** is when one uses strategy to gain power. Too much time is spent interpreting other people's motives and trying to read hidden agendas.

4. **Disengagement** is when people are still getting paid even though they "clocked-out" years ago. They will put in the minimal effort required to get their pay check.

5. **Turnover** results when the best performers in an organization choose to leave an organization in pursuit of a job where they are seen as trusted and a contributor adding value.

6. **Churn** is the effort and costs associated with constantly having to find new customers, suppliers, distributors, and investors because there is a lack of loyalty.

7. **Fraud** is flat-out dishonesty. Fraud is a circular tax; when companies tighten the reigns to prevent fraud they reduce their fraud-related losses, but they inevitably see an increase in the other six areas.

If trust reduces transaction costs, what can companies do to build trust in their relationships?

## BUILDING TRUST

The key to finding and establishing trust in any partnership is to discover the right formula for the partnership. Is it built over time? Does one person choose to trust his partner? Or is trust built quickly out of necessity and put to the test? Typically, trust is formed over time. It need not take years to create high levels of trust, however. High degrees of trust can be developed rather quickly when circumstances demand it. There are powerful ways to form trust. Below are six proven ways to increase trust in your business relationships.

### Choosing Trust

First and foremost, to trust or not is a *choice*. Parties choose to trust each other and act in a trustworthy manner or not. It is that simple. It is also a choice to expect that others will act only in their own self-interest without regard for another's interests. Likewise, it is a choice to expect that partners will act in the best interests of the partnership. A business partner may provide a reason not to trust—but it is imperative that the parties purposely start by setting the tone that trust is a key factor to the mutual success of their relationship.

Trust is the result of actions, and since actions are a result of human thought and willpower, individuals and organizations can make a choice to take actions that increase trust and avoid actions that decrease trust. Trust goes to the heart of the collaborative partnership. And it must be established once and for all: trust does not increase or decrease by coincidence.

Dell and GENCO ATC are good examples of business partners that choose to pursue a path of trust to help them transform their relationship. Dell and GENCO ATC—Dell's repair and returns service provider—had worked together since 2005. While GENCO ATC's performance was good, the relationship was nevertheless strained. Laboring under Dell's "every dollar every year" procurement mantra meant that GENCO ATC felt it could no longer reduce costs while maintaining a high service level and profitability. Rather than keep pushing on costs, in 2011 Dell and GENCO ATC modified how they viewed the business, seeking to shift from a WIIFMe mindset to a WIIFWe mindset. They decided to transition the relationship using the University of Tennessee's Vested methodology.

The parties met on neutral ground at the Texas Motor Speedway during the dog days of a hot August summer to discuss the future of their relationship. The negotiations were so tense at times that Dell and GENCO ATC attendees went to separate rooms to cool off. Tom Perry, GENCO ATC's president of reverse logistics later recalled, "There was a moment of truth in that June meeting. I did not want to proceed because I didn't have enough trust [in Dell] to move forward." But it was during those cooling off periods that his peers at GENCO ATC convinced Perry to stay the course to negotiate a collaborative partnership agreement with Dell. Perry later said: "I had an epiphany. If you can't get past absence of trust, you can't ever make it work. I can't say enough about how that's changed everything."[6]

The parties took a leap of faith to trust and went on to establish a collaborative Vested partnership. "There was a recognition for the importance of the relationship and most important for the power of trust," Perry explained. He proudly added, "Today, the atmosphere at our meetings is 180 degrees different from the past."[7]

Trust has the power to transform relationships. Within six months of signing the new partnership agreement, the companies achieved record-setting results, including reducing scrap by 62 percent. "The results have been beyond my wildest dreams," said Stephen McPherson, Dell's global operations Senior leader. "It has simply been amazing to see how we could literally turn around the culture and see such drastic results in such a short time frame."[8] That is the definition of win-win, made possible by the choice to trust. Perry made the decision to trust without Dell first earning his trust. That moment changed everything for Dell and GENCO ATC.

## Do What It Takes to Not Lose Trust

Once formed trust can quickly fade. Trust is fragile and is easily damaged or destroyed. And once destroyed, it is often harder to rebuild trust than it was to establish it in the first place. The path to trust can be long. The path from trust to mistrust is almost always short.

McDonald's has long been known for building long-term and trusting relationships with its suppliers. Unfortunately, sometimes suppliers do things that lose trust. When Devin Cole, group vice president of the food service division of Tyson Foods, was tapped for the lead role in managing the McDonald's account, Tyson Foods was not in a favored status. Cole explained how Tyson's management lost McDonald's trust for a time. "Trust is the basic building block of McDonald's supplier relationships and is a fragile thing that can be eroded through the actions of a single individual if not relentlessly protected. Tyson has been a longtime supplier of McDonald's, but new leadership in our company managed—or, more appropriately, mismanaged—the McDonald's account. Tyson started to treat McDonald's like every other customer, and the magic dissipated as the fundamentals of trust and collaboration were lost with Tyson's management turnover. Tyson got complacent as a supplier, and our performance slipped."[9]

Reflecting on how Tyson lost McDonald's trust for a time, Cole explained, "It was us that had gotten off track. McDonald's consistently adhered to their values and rewards. They held themselves accountable and remained open to talking with us, even when we weren't holding up our end. McDonald's always had a willingness to meet with me and coach me on how Tyson could get back on a path to mutual success."[10]

## Create a Shadow of the Future for the Relationship

In chapter 1, we shared Robert Axelrod's pioneering study into the nature of collaboration. Axelrod promoted a concept called the shadow of the future.[11] The shadow of the future means "that the importance of the next encounter between the same two individuals must be great enough to make defection unprofitable [...].[12] If the shadow of the future looms large enough—organizations believe that they will meet again—they are more likely to build a trusting relationship. The future starts to influence the behavior of how parties behave in the present, and organizations will promote building trust in a relationship as a mechanism to establish stability and harmony in a relationship that must be functional in the future. Simply put, most people and organizations will act with integrity and trust if they know they have to work together the next day.

Trust is essential when there are uncertainties in the future. And as we know, the future is always uncertain. In theory there is an indefinite number of possible futures, but in order to be able to make plans and act upon them, people and companies must bet on some of those possible futures. Without that bet, we are doomed to passivity. The problem is that the future cannot be controlled. In a business relationship it is easy to become wary because companies do not know if their business partners will make the same decisions and take the same actions as they might. Although there is the expectation, fear, or hope that some things will occur and that other things will not occur, that the other party will do some things and avoid doing others, there is no way to know for sure. Will they be loyal to the partnership? Will they do what they say they will do?

Trust relieves the future of some of this uncertainty between partners. In a situation characterized by high trust *and* trustworthiness, partners will have enough mutual confidence to continue to collaborate in a constructive way. This certainty allows them to make plans and act upon them, to bet on the future.

While the future is always uncertain, trust reduces complexity and improves confidence as the parties work together on their path to the future. With trust in place, an individual or organization will plan for the future and act upon those plans, rather than wasting time obsessing over what *might* happen. Further, trust allows partners some measure of flexibility if and when something unexpected does happen. Trust simplifies the world in a way that lets individuals and organizations make and execute plans that lead to growth and joint value creation.

## Develop a Culture of Accountability

A basic rule for building trust is to state intentions and then follow through with action. This is, however, not enough. In addition, a culture of accountability is needed in the partnership. If one of the partners fails to be trustworthy or to show trust, the partners must raise that for discussion and not hide it. This means calling out behavior that undermines trust. If the one partner violates the other's trust, such as taking advantage of a situation, it is imperative that the non-violating partner discuss the untrustworthy behavior. Such a breach of trust cannot be water cooler gossip or fodder to assail the partner months after the fact. Each partner owes it to the other to hold each other (and themselves) accountable in a timely manner. Otherwise, people will start to question their partner's intentions and possibly provide justification for their own untrustworthy behavior, triggering a negative tit-for-tat game.

## Leave Money on the Table

Oliver Williamson—the 2009 Nobel laureate in economic sciences and pioneer in the research of transaction cost economics—promotes the concept of *leaving money on the table* as a way to build trust.[13] Williamson notes, "Always leaving money on the table can...be interpreted as a signal of constructive intent to work cooperatively, thereby to assuage concerns over relentlessly calculative strategic behavior."[14] On one hand, the party leaving the money shows that it is trustworthy by refusing to act for short-term gain. On the other hand, the same party shows that it trusts the other party not to "take the money and run." When the other party does not take the money off the table, that party is being trustworthy.

Unfortunately, many practitioners scoff at the idea of leaving money on the table. Some of these practitioners are viewed as leaders in the industry. One such individual, a director of contract management for a very large company, participated in a panel at an industry conference with his peers. Unfortunately, this director was not aware of Williamson's scholarly insights. While on the panel he proclaimed, "Don't leave money on the table. When you do, you leave value for your company on the table." This kind of opportunistic thinking is deeply ingrained in many procurement and negotiation professionals and reinforces the usual low-cost, transaction-based mentality that dominates many contract negotiations.

## Use a Credible Negotiating Style

Another notable way Williamson recommends to build trust is to steer away from a "muscular" negotiation style and instead use a credible negotiation style. Williamson describes the muscular style of contracting as power ploys used by one company to extort concessions from the other company. While buyers or suppliers can be more powerful in a relationship, it is often the buying company that wields the power. After all, the golden rule in business usually is: he who holds the gold rules.

Williamson correctly points out that companies that use the muscular approach use up their suppliers in a "myopic and inefficient" approach to contracting.[15] Examples of this trust-busting style abound. For example, many buying companies use their power to bid every dollar every year, despite outstanding performance by a service provider. Or a service provider will intentionally low-ball the price for services only to flex its muscle later to make up the difference in expensive change orders.

Williamson urges individuals and organizations to use what he terms as a credible style—one that is described as "hardheaded and wise." Negotiators should not be mean-spirited but rather strive for clear results and accountability. Wise negotiators recognize that business is dynamic and contracts are "incomplete and thus pose cooperative adaptation needs."[16] In other words, credible negotiators are forward thinking (and acting), uncovering potential risks, and developing a mechanism to address these factors and then factoring them into the contract.

## ASSESSING THE TWO SIDES OF TRUST

Trust creates commitment and as such has two sides. First, trust obliges the partners *to act in a trusting manner*, that is, they proactively create a positive environment that builds confidence and establishes expectations for how partners treat each other. Second, trust obliges the partners to *treat each other as being trustworthy*, that is, they believe that the other party will keep promises, fulfill its contractual obligations, and act in accordance with agreed upon principles of behavior.

The ideal situation for getting to a WIIFWe mindset is when partners are both trusting *and* trustworthy. Unfortunately, most individuals and organizations do not have a good grasp on whether they are worthy of their counterpart's trust. After all, who would suggest they are *not* trustworthy? For this reason, look in the mirror.

### Assessing Your Own Trustworthiness

In his 1987 megahit "Man in the Mirror," pop singer Michael Jackson sang: "I am starting with the man in the mirror."[17] That is where the process of creating trust must start—with the man or woman in the mirror. The negotiator or negotiation team must first and foremost ask, "Do I, based on how I have been acting in the past, deserve to be trusted by others?" Or does our company deserve to be trusted, given our past behavior?

Trust requires a degree of faith that others will act in the best interest of the partnership. It is easy, when thinking about trust, to look at how others behave. People may even ask themselves, "How can we possibly trust them? Every time we share some valuable information or make a concession of some sort, they take advantage of us and abuse our trust!"

Interestingly, your partner may think the same thing about you. Living in that vicious circle, people look for reasons not to trust each other. Both partners expect that others will fail to be trustworthy.

The only way to break out of this vicious circle is to start with yourself. It is impossible to force others to be trustworthy. It is only possible to affect their trustworthiness by being trustworthy in your own communications and actions. Therefore, establishing trust starts by asking the following questions:

**How Trustworthy Are You?**

- How do you define trustworthiness?
- In what ways do you act in a trustworthy manner?
- What challenges to trustworthiness do you face?
- What excuses do you make about not being trustworthy?
- Do you clearly communicate your intentions and then follow up by fulfilling your promises?
- Do you act with integrity? (Can individuals and organizations depend upon you to act consistently with how you acted in the past?)

When an *organization* asks itself these questions, it must also acknowledge that an organization consists of the actions of many different individuals and that all of them must act in a consistent manner if the organization wants to appear trustworthy. If an organization wants to build trustworthy relationships with others, it is therefore necessary that it ask the following questions:

**How Trustworthy Is Your Organization?**

- Who (list names) in our organization do our partners need to trust?
- Who (list names) in our organization can damage trust by acting inconsistently with our declared motives and intentions?
- Among those employees identified—who might damage trust and/or act in an untrustworthy manner? Why?

## Assess Your Perceptions of Your Partner's Trustworthiness

Once you've assessed your or your organization's trustworthiness, look at your perceptions of the other party's trustworthiness. This is easier in an existing relationship than in a new relationship. If you don't have an ongoing relationship, you'll have to get other people's perceptions. Perhaps you could interview your potential partner's partners. Or you could interview your potential partner by modifying the questions to reflect a self-assessment of its trustworthiness. Naturally, a new partner will want to gloss over any issues about being trustworthy. The answers are not nearly as important as the questions you ask and the other party's willingness to engage in a conversation about trust.

It's important to assess your perception of your partner's trustworthiness periodically throughout the relationship. When assessing the other party's trustworthiness, ask the following questions:

### How Trustworthy Is Your Partner?

- How do they define trustworthiness? Is it similar to our definition?
- Do we have any reasons not to trust them? What are those reasons?
- Did we contribute in any way to their untrustworthy behavior?
- Have they said one thing and done another thing in the past? What was the impact on our end?
- Have they had opportunities to act in their own short-term self-interest without doing it?
- Do different individuals in their organization show different degrees of trustworthiness? Who? How should we address that issue?

What if you doubt your partner's trustworthiness? When this happens we recommend that you actively discuss the trust issue with your partner. It is possible to say, for example: "We have been thinking: As you know, we feel it is important that we have a relationship based on mutual trust. We think it would help build trust if we could talk about trust. You may have some doubts about our trustworthiness, and if you do, we would like you to tell us. And we would like to discuss with you some issues that affect our trust in you. Would that be ok?" You are inviting your partner to discuss this foundational issue. And then based on the discussion, you have a choice to make.

## The Compatibility and Trust Assessment

Accurately assessing trust is not easy. It is often a one-sided affair. In other words, a buying company will evaluate a supplier's trustworthiness without understanding the supplier's perceptions of the buying company's trustworthiness. Rather than rely on such a one-sided point of view, professors Gerald Ledlow and Karl Manrodt developed the Compatibility and Trust Assessment™ (CaT) to measure the strength of a business relationship across five dimensions. Trust is the first dimension. The other four dimensions are discussed in chapter 3. The CaT defines trust as "the consistency of actions and words over time that focuses on mutual benefit of the parties. Trust is the foundation of the relationship."[18]

The CaT achieves what a self-assessment cannot: a 360-degree view. For instance, the buyer assesses its trustworthiness and its perceptions of the supplier. The supplier likewise assesses its trustworthiness and its perceptions of the buyer. The scores reveal alignment or a lack of alignment between the companies. If the buyer (or supplier) perceives itself as trustworthy but its counterpart does not share that perception, there is a problem. The parties will have to address these differences in perceptions before continuing on the path to the We mindset.

While answering the questions above will give readers an initial impression of their trustworthiness and that of their partner, the most effective way to gauge trustworthiness is to complete a 360-degree assessment such as the CaT.

## Improve Your Trustworthiness

Building trustworthiness starts with declaring how to act and then following through. Nothing builds trustworthiness better and faster than when words and actions coincide. Trust is built when people know each other's intentions, motivations, and agendas. Unfortunately, when intentions are unknown, it is easy to fall into the trap of projecting our worst fears onto other's actions whether they deserve it or not. We want our partners to declare what they intend to do; but we must first do so ourselves. To build trust it is important to say things such as:

- "We want a trusting relationship and will trust you not to abuse our trust in you."

- "We will, in the negotiation process and for the term of our relationship, act in accordance with our set of guiding principles."
- "If we have the benefit of being better informed, we will be transparent, thus allowing you to make better decisions."

Declaring how you will act is meaningless unless there is also follow through. Nothing ruins trust faster than *not acting* in accordance with declared intentions.

For example, recently a buyer contracting for complex mobile services expressed an intention to carry out the negotiations in a fair and equitable manner. The supplier expressed similar intentions, and for a time the negotiations were transparent, honest, and efficient.

A few days before the deal was expected to close, however, external circumstances altered the relative bargaining power of the parties, clearly giving the buyer the upper hand. At first negotiators from the companies acted according to previously stated intentions. But the buyer's attorney had a different set of intentions than his teammates. The attorney started to use the increased bargaining power to alter parts of the contract that were already agreed upon. The attorney's actions created a serious crisis of trust in the relationship.

Although the buyer's CEO claimed that the attorney had not acted on his instructions, the supplier's trust in the buyer was severely damaged because the attorney had decided not to act in line with the buyer's expressed intentions. It took time for the partners to reestablish trust and close the deal. It is important to reestablish trust when one person damages trust (whether intentionally or not). More important, explain to your colleagues the importance of acting with integrity as an *organization*.

## Treat the Others as Trustworthy

Having focused on the first side of trust—your own trustworthiness—you then begin to focus on the other side: to show trust and treat the others as trustworthy. The rule here is the same: make statements and actions regarding trust coincide. First, declare that you will show trust and then, second, follow through.

It is important to tell your partners that you intend to trust them until they do something that is not trustworthy. Therefore, expressing an intention to trust the other party is an important element in building trust. For example, a company could say at the initial stage of a negotiation: "We want to tell you that we place great value in trust. We know and feel that trust is maybe the most important thing for our collaboration to succeed. Therefore, we will be trustworthy in this process; we will trust you and treat you as worthy of our trust. We expect you not to take advantage of the trust we give you." The following example demonstrates this concept.

An artist contacted a record company to inquire about the record company's interest in releasing his new album. The record company recognized this as a good opportunity and wanted to enter into negotiations with the artist. The record company did not want to spend time and resources negotiating an agreement only to find out later that the artist preferred to work with another record company that could offer the artist a better deal.

When initiating the contract negotiations, the record company said to the artist: "We want to release your record and we are willing to negotiate a contract with you. However, we want to be clear that we do not want to waste our time negotiating just to find you will go to someone else. We will provide you with a good and fair offer that is mutually beneficial. In return, *we trust that you will not negotiate with another record company*." The artist agreed and the contract was closed in a matter of days. The record was a big hit, making a lot of money for the record company and the artist.

A key to success here was that the record company expressed its intent to trust the artist and at the same time also expressed its expectation that the artist would not violate the trust. Expressing trusting expectations and intentions often has important psychological consequences. Simply put: *no one wants to be caught being untrustworthy*. In most societies, if not all, the consequence of failing to be trustworthy is loss of honor and prestige. A man or woman you cannot trust is not a man or woman of honor. Although honor in many societies has less importance today than historically, it still plays an important role.

Simply expressing intentions without the corresponding actions is worthless. It is common for companies to pay lip service to their partner by declaring an intention to trust. For example, a buyer might tell an important supplier it trusts that supplier, only to set down in detail exactly what the supplier may and may not do during the contract period. Such detailed instructions signal distrust, which is even more damaging to the relationship after the customer has expressed its intent to show trust.

Another aspect of showing that you trust your partner is *to not assume the worst in people*. For example, if you followed Williamson's advice to leave money on the table, do not anticipate and act as if the other party will take the money and run. In effect you are saying, "I know that you have the possibility to serve your own short-term interest now. I know that you also have strong incentives to do so. But I trust that you will not take advantage of the situation and will be trustworthy."

## IS YOUR RELATIONSHIP TRUSTING ENOUGH?

Take a moment to determine whether your relationship or potential relationship has enough trust to continue on the Getting to We process. Establishing an atmosphere of trust is absolutely critical to the success of a highly collaborative relationship. If trust is lacking for any reason, take the time now to build (or rebuild) trust. If there is sufficient trust to continue on the journey, there remain two other foundational elements that must be in place before parties begin to negotiate the relationship.

# CHAPTER 3

# TRANSPARENCY AND COMPATIBILITY

While trust is a key quality needed for any highly collaborative relationship to succeed, it is not the only quality. The parties also need a foundation built upon transparency and compatibility.

Transparency requires that parties share relevant information to ensure they will make good decisions for themselves *and* for the relationship. It also includes an aspect of personal openness. Personal openness is the degree of comfort people have about sharing more personal concerns, motivations, wants, and needs within the relationship.

Compatibility describes the extent of the parties' fit. In other words, is there a good corporate cultural fit or not? If not, how can the parties still work together effectively?

These two elements can build or undermine trust. Each party should understand the level of transparency and compatibility needed to foster trust and complete the foundation building process started in chapter 2.

## TRANSPARENCY

Solving dynamic business problems requires parties to share more information than they ever imagined possible. Truly collaborative relationships embrace this and work to determine what information to share, how much information to share, and with whom to share it.

Transparency is the open and timely sharing of all information relevant to a party's ability to make wise decisions for itself and the partnership. Transparency is one of the three foundational elements on the path to get to We because it fosters trust and generates an environment for reaching more holistic solutions. Transparency should never be a buzzword; unfortunately, people will say they are transparent, but often there is little meaning behind the word.

## Transparency Fosters Trust

Trust and transparency go hand-in-hand. The more parties trust, the more comfortable they feel sharing information. More transparency helps build more trust.

Business people often wonder whether sharing information can change the conversation. Absolutely. A vice president for commercial management for a major outsourcing provider said, "Some of the most successful resolutions [to a negotiation] have been when there is nothing left to hide. Openness clearly leads to more value, yet often it takes a crisis to make it happen."[1] With transparency, partners begin to have a more rational, fact-based conversation. They no longer use information as leverage to use against the partner.

***Sharing Information Pays Off***
In 2010 Sykes, a global leader in providing customer contact management solutions and services in the business process outsourcing (BPO) arena, was renegotiating an outsourcing agreement with one of its partners. Like most traditional negotiations, the negotiations centered on money. Sykes' client, a financial institution, wanted to expand its business with Sykes because of Sykes' high-quality service but simultaneously assumed that Sykes was making an unfairly high profit from them.

Together, Sykes and the client decided to approach their negotiations from a WIIFWe perspective. With the guiding influence of a WIIFWe mindset, the tenor and context for the negotiations changed over time. Jim Hobby, recently retired executive vice president of global operations for Sykes, cites the power that transparency brought to one of Sykes's most strategic client accounts: "It was through open communication that we could move down a path that could lead to better outcomes for both of us. I realized that a win-win was not just a buzzword, but was something that really was possible."[2]

At one point in the negotiations, Hobby came to a significant real-ization. Both companies were laboring under some serious misconcep-tions that tainted the conversations and limited their ability to see the larger picture.

For many months, the financial institution expressed concern that it did not want Sykes to take advantage by making more profit from their account than Sykes was making on other accounts. Hobby knew that the typical profit margins in the industry were in the 8–10 percent range. Sykes was not making that at some of its client's locations. Hobby explained, "Sykes is a public company and has an obligation to its share-holders. The client wanted us to expand in an area, but it was not finan-cially viable for Sykes. Before we made the decision to be transparent, we seemed to be at a crossroads in our discussions."

Because Sykes decided to embrace a WIIFWe mindset, Sykes felt that it needed to share more information than it would have tradition-ally shared so its client could make a better informed decision. Hobby said, "We agreed to model the business at various locations that per-formed the client's work. We looked at Sykes's company-wide financial objectives and how the client's work compared to Sykes's company-wide goals. By addressing our client's concern head-on in a transparent man-ner it helped us view our business through a new lens."

At first, this level of transparency felt risky. A colleague of Hobby's warned him, "Sharing this financial information is like sharing on Facebook. Once we post on the wall we cannot take it down." Many at Sykes wondered how the client would receive the information and how it would use the information going forward. Nevertheless, Hobby and his team felt that sharing the information would benefit the partnership and trusted their client not to abuse Sykes's trust by using the informa-tion against Sykes.

Sykes's willingness to be transparent paid off. The client was recep-tive to the information and to having a dialogue with Sykes about the operating income percentage points at various locations. By sharing information with the intent to help the client make an informed deci-sion, Sykes showed the client that Sykes was not trying to take advantage of its client. Hobby noted, "Sharing the financial information brought business logic to the conversation. It was a breakthrough point for all of us. Our client realized Sykes was being honest with them." The client

saw in numbers what Hobby had been saying for months and agreed
to a price increase at some locations to keep Sykes operating at those
locations.

Looking back at the negotiations, Hobby noted, "There was nothing
wrong with being more open and sharing some financial information so
that we could partner in a more trusting environment. Nothing we did
put Sykes at risk. It was all in the spirit of good faith and contributed to
an open and honest dialogue with the client…openness made our conversations business discussions. The conversations were more rational."

### Better Solutions

Transparently sharing information that can enable better decision making and solution development lies at the heart of human progress and
economic wealth. Research shows that when negotiators fail to reach
a well-balanced agreement it is often because they failed to exchange
enough information to allow each other to identify options.[3] Effective
information flow promotes more balanced agreements—and more
important, better solutions.

Another example comes from a $3.5 billion company that had expe-
rienced years of contentious conversations with one of its strategic suppliers. Because the supplier was so strategically important, the company
could not easily move to greener pastures with a new supplier. A key
area of frustration was a perceived lack of innovation by the supplier.
The company needed to make a bold move to prove that it was really
going to treat its service provider as a strategic business partner rather
than as a simple commodity provider. At the outset of conversations to
renew the service provider's agreement, the company agreed to give the
service provider its master agreement with its customer (the end user).
The company felt it had nothing to hide and everything to gain by allowing its service provider—a recognized expert in the area—to generate
value-creating ideas. And it worked. Conversations shifted from how to
penalize for performance errors to measures designed to catch and rec-
tify problems before the customer was ever aware of them, thus creating
a win for all concerned.

Companies often loathe sharing information with their business
partners. Many companies are reluctant to share information about
internal strategies, coordination efforts, and pending reorganizations.

Others generally don't share internal coordination problems that would impact a service provider's staffing decisions. Yet, internal issues at the buying company can often impact the service provider's staffing decisions, which in turn impact the nature of the relationship and the quantity and quality of services provided. Not only does withholding information affect the service provider's performance, it also sows the seeds of mistrust later in the relationship.

In addition to the more typical kinds of information companies can share with each other, organizations should share what most negotiators would never disclose: their BATNA (Best Alternative to a Negotiated Agreement). Many popular negotiation authors advise negotiators to develop a strong BATNA but never reveal it to their counterpart. However, research shows that negotiators who were aware of and shared their BATNA took less extreme positions, made better trade-offs and *increased the size of the pie* as compared to those who did not share their BATNA.[4] Why? The old adage says that information is power—and most negotiators are paranoid that their business partner will take advantage of them if they show their cards.

### Information Is Power

When people say information is power, often what they really mean is that the *unequal access to information* creates a power imbalance. In a world in which unequal access to information is power, most people tend to hide information, hoard information, misrepresent information, and most of all, use information as a battering ram to get their way.

Information is so powerful because people accumulate information with a desire to present that information to support their own agenda. People want to change another person's point of view. This is not bad per se—if enough of the right kind of information is shared with good intentions.

Too often people succumb to the temptation to share only information that bolsters their position or that undermines their counterpart's position, while concealing information that exposes a weakness. This is a classic WIIFMe tactic. The intentional concealment of some information skews other people's ability to make good decisions. It is also reinforces people's beliefs that they cannot trust anyone at the bargaining table.

Complete sharing is powerful because it builds trust. With a We mentality, partners share all relevant information to help them make an informed decision. Information really is power if the sharing of information is approached with the right mindset. Jim Hobby shared a complete financial model, not just the part of the model that showed breakeven or net loss locations. Sykes and its client enjoyed a more trusting relationship as a result.

More important, sharing information becomes the primary medium for creating a common definition of the situation or a common picture of a current condition or situation. Commonality can also serve to provide a rationale to change or modify a position or a course of action while allowing people to save face.

## Personal Openness

Transparency comes in two forms: sharing information and personal openness. Each plays an important role in forming the environment for fostering trust. While most business people understand the nature of sharing information, they don't often recognize the importance of personal openness in decision making.

Personal openness refers to a person's comfort level in disclosing information such as concerns, motivations, wants, needs, and goals and how they can play out in the partnership. Personal openness also refers to a person's comfort in allowing others to disclose similar information.

In this context, openness is important because it relates to business people's comfort with telling the truth about how issues, problems, and situations will really impact them and their team. In an environment of little openness, people will often consider things that they are unwilling to express. Environments that discourage openness run the risk that people will fail to disclose the potential impact of decisions, which in turn allows for poor decision making. This tendency not to share is exacerbated in traditional customer/vendor relationships. Service providers will keep mum about the impacts of decisions out of fear that they'll be shot down by their customers.

James Tamm and Ronald Luyet, authors of *Radical Collaboration*, state, "We do have a strong bias about the advantages of increasing openness if your goal is to build more effective relationships. Problem solving and relationship building almost always benefit from increased openness."[5] Therefore people who want greater collaboration have to start by being open, and that means sharing.

## What Should You Share?

There is no correct answer to the question of what to share. Parties that sincerely want to adopt a WIIFWe mindset should share information relevant to the decisions that need to be made. Typically, this is often exponentially more than is being shared in most relationships. Obviously, there will be information that is not shared. However, choosing to share the right information is critical for fostering trust.

When in doubt, companies should consider the following litmus test. If the business partner asks for certain information, assume the request is with good intentions. Concerns about risks associated with transparency can be handled through nondisclosure agreements entered into at the beginning of the negotiation, obliging the parties not to disclose any transferred information to third parties unless agreed in advance.

Advice on building effective coalitions is relevant to a discussion on what to share. When building an effective coalition, it is wise to share everything you know in order to maximize what others in the coalition know. This free flow of relevant information creates a common pool of knowledge that increases people's ability to arrive at a solution that is *in their individual and collective best interests.* For example, collaborative negotiators have chosen to share the following:

**Could you share?**

- The whole budget not just part of it and complete financial data when developing a dynamic pricing model
- Objectives and their corresponding importance to the organization
- Accurate forecasts and projections
- Details regarding strategic initiatives
- Potential problems, issues, or concerns
- Changes in policies, regulations, or personnel

- Organizational goals and targets
- Your Best Alternative To a Negotiated Agreement (BATNA)

It is common for the more powerful party, whether internal department or external provider, to expect the less powerful party to share this information. But embracing a WIIFWe mindset is a two-way street. For this reason, organizations that are sincere about creating a highly collaborative relationship built on a WIIFWe mindset will openly share information even though they could use their power to justify withholding information.

Many companies find it helpful to consider the following issues when considering what to share and with whom.

### Questions to Ask Yourself

- Can your partner be trusted not to abuse your trust by using the information to gain an advantage at your expense?
- What can I share that will bring value to the relationship and build trust?
- Will the information foster transparency and encourage better decision making?
- Are there any potential negative consequences (privacy or regulatory issues)?
- Who should be consulted before sharing information?
- Who should approve the decision and the nature of the information?
- Does your partner have appropriate confidentiality policies and practices in place to prevent the dissemination of information beyond the intended recipients?
- If we cannot, or will not, share some information (specific financial data, for example), is there alternative data that we can share that will still promote trust, honesty, and better decision making?

Finally, once the decision is made to share information, it is important to share more extensively and earlier in the process than in a more conventional negotiation. This is especially true when sharing information regarding personnel or organizational realignment or potential problems. Parties should be warned early enough to allow them time to plan for the situation.

Ultimately, the parties are developing the conditions for a free and open discussion of all related issues and concerns. Planting the seeds of transparency will become even more critical for those partnerships that negotiate financial aspects of the relationship.

Transparency is the second foundational element needed to begin on the journey to We. Compatibility is the third and final element of a strong foundation for a highly collaborative relationship.

## COMPATIBILITY

While trust and transparency are important foundational components for creating a WIIFWe mindset *compatibility* also matters, although to a lesser degree. Successful partnerships do not need to have nearly as much cultural compatibility as trust and transparency. At least one research study found that when there was little compatibility among team members, the teams that designed a fair and transparent communication process circumvented problems associated with low compatibility.[6]

But what exactly is cultural compatibility? Many refer to cultural compatibility as "fit."

### Cultural Fit

With respect to a cultural fit, the parties should have enough commonality to foster an atmosphere of trust, which in turn will allow the openness necessary to solve problems. If the partners are new to the relationship or if they are not entirely compatible, they should establish a communication framework that fosters transparency and a fair process for making decisions. In the research study noted above, when teams were formed quickly and without time to evaluate compatibility among the members, those teams still performed at a high level when there was a fair and transparent process for making decisions.

*A Good Fit*

In 2003 Procter & Gamble (P&G) decided to outsource several operational functions, including facilities management. Jones Lang LaSalle
(JLL), a global leader in real estate and facilities management services,
was selected as the best partner to manage the transformation of P&G's
facilities and real estate portfolio in more than 60 countries.

William Reeves, P&G's corporate real estate leader, led the outsourcing efforts in facilities management. P&G set out to identify the
best-in-breed partner.

When the potential list was narrowed to a handful of applicants,
P&G created a unique next step. Suppliers were asked to conduct three-
day site visits at five locations around the world. The prospective firms'
assignment was to study the sites, understand the P&G business, and
develop a five-year plan describing what they would do to manage the
business if awarded the contract.

From the very beginning, JLL knew that P&G would be a good
client and took the assignment seriously. Lauralee Martin, JLL's chief
executive officer of the Americas (formerly chief operating officer/chief
financial officer), recognized the "chemistry" between each company's
corporate culture from the beginning.

When P&G selected JLL as its service provider, Reeves recognized JLL's competence in facilities management, and he saw the
value in cultural fit. During the supplier selection process, Reeves
noticed when the JLL and P&G teams met together for key meetings, it was hard to tell who worked for which company. Reeves noted,
"JLL was a good fit...P&G and JLL shared something even more
important—similar corporate ethics and commitments."[7] A comparison of company values validated the similarities in cultures, as seen
in figure 3.1.

When Reeves met with Bill Thummel, the JLL global account
executive, to let him know that P&G had made the decision to go
with JLL, Reeves shook hands with Thummel to symbolically seal
the deal, stating, "We know that you [JLL] and the other suppliers
we evaluated have never done this before, and neither have we. But
JLL has the culture that is much like P&G's. We think we have the
best chance of being successful with you because you are so much
like us."

Figure 3.1   Comparison of P&G and Jones Lang LaSalle corporate cultures

| Stated Principle/Value Category | P&G | Jones Lang LaSalle |
|---|---|---|
| Workplace | We attract and recruit the finest people in the world. We build our organization from within, promoting and rewarding people without regard to any difference unrelated to performance. | We strive to attract and retain the most talented individuals, encouraging and enabling them to succeed. We foster an inclusive environment that values the richness of our differences and reflects the diverse world in which we work. |
| Community | P&G and its employees have a long-standing commitment to being good citizens and neighbors in all the places where we do business around the world. | We endeavor to be good citizens wherever we live and work. |
| Ethics and Corporate Governance | P&G has been built through the character of its people.<br>    That character is reflected in the Company's Values, which have been fundamental to our success for more than 175 years. Our continued success depends on each one of us doing our part to uphold these values in our day-to-day work and in all the decisions we make. | We are proud of our global reputation for uncompromising integrity, ethical conduct and corporate governance. Our Code of Business Ethics and Vendor Code of Conduct are followed by our own employees and everyone who does business on behalf of our firm. We are also proud of the rigor and quality of the firm's corporate governance and the benefits these policies produce for our stakeholders. |

*Misfits*

While P&G and JLL had a good cultural fit, some organizations have cultures that simply do not lend themselves to healthy external relationships. Companies and their suppliers or service providers should be proactive in determining if they have a good cultural fit. This isn't a case of right or wrong, it is merely the need to admit that successful long-term relationships require empathy and concern for each other that will not be achieved if there is a cultural mismatch.

One such company was a pharmaceutical company that outsourced its facilities and real estate management (for clarification, the service provider involved was not JLL). Both companies were very frustrated with their existing relationship. A significant reason for the discontent was a lack of compatibility between the two companies' corporate cultures. The pharmaceutical company's corporate culture was very creative and innovative. It placed a lot of weight on creativity and thus valued flexibility with a high tolerance for constant change—almost to the point of the company seeming to have attention deficit disorder. On the other hand, the service provider's company was founded by engineers. Its corporate culture was steeped in process rigor. It disliked change. Change agents were seen as threatening. The service provider effectively shut down the company's frequent requests for change in the name of "efficiencies" and process standardization. There was a genuine culture clash.

All the varying aspects of corporate culture are not explored here. There are hundreds of resources available with that information. We do however want to focus on one aspect: a full 360-degree awareness of each party's compatibility with the other party.

## Awareness

Awareness is invaluable. Companies that don't understand their own values, intentions, and patterns, find themselves flitting from fire to fire, which gives them little control over their own destiny. They are also less likely to understand what kinds of companies will have the best cultural fit. The authors of *Radical Collaboration* explain, "If you want to improve a relationship or change the culture of an entire organization, the first step is to increase people's self-awareness."[8] So, begin by assessing compatibility, which in turn leads to more awareness and control.

*The Compatibility and Trust Assessment*

As mentioned in chapter 2, individuals in existing external relationships find it valuable to assess the levels of trust, innovation, communication, team orientation, and focus. The Compatibility and Trust™ Assessment (CaT) was developed by professors Gerald Ledlow and Karl Manrodt to measure the strength of business relationships across five dimensions:

- **Trust:** Trust is the consistency of actions and words over time that focuses on the mutual benefit of the parties. Trust is the foundation of the relationship.
- **Innovation:** Innovation is an organization's ability to dynamically deal with change and its tolerance for risk and trying out new ideas and solutions. Strong and trusting relationships allow the parties to share risks and rewards, investing in each other's capabilities and collaborating to achieve common goals.
- **Communication:** Communication is the efficient and effective transfer of meaning through words and actions to achieve and grow mutually beneficial outcomes. The open and timely sharing of all information that is relevant to a partner's decision-making ability.
- **Team Orientation:** Team orientation is the ability to focus and direct individual goals and objectives into a cohesive group strategy. Team orientation is the enabler and drives compatibility.
- **Focus:** Focus is the ability to combine individual roles into a corporate direction for the benefit of all stakeholders. There is common purpose and direction. A common strategic focus on innovation drives value in the relationship.[9]

A company's culture is made up of these five dimensions. The dynamics of how each organization aligns its behaviors on each of the five dimensions can strengthen—or weaken—the health of a relationship. A healthy relationship is aware of how well the organizations align and actively strive to close the gaps in order to mitigate opportunism and promote collaboration.

The CaT scores the buyer on its perception of itself and its perception of the supplier. Likewise, the CaT scores the supplier on its perception of itself and its perception of the buyer. This provides a global view of the relationship dynamics and organizational alignment across the five dimensions. The assessment looks at attributes that are important to supporting collaborative relationships. If the cultural fit between the companies has a large degree of misalignment, this often impacts the partners' ability to establish a WIIFWe mindset.

By comparing self-views and perceptions of the other party the assessment can determine how well the organizations are aligned. Misalignments can often be addressed and repaired. The discussions are often revealing, and the process of opening up and putting issues on the table builds better, more trusting relationships.

Misalignment of cultures results in increased transaction costs, limited solutions, and fewer options to build value in the relationship. Alignment of cultures builds value and results in decreased transaction costs, broader solutions and agreements, and more options for innovation, as shown in the value map in figure 3.2.

The value map is used to plot the relationship by the five relationship dynamics (behaviors of trust, innovation, communication,

Figure 3.2  Value Map

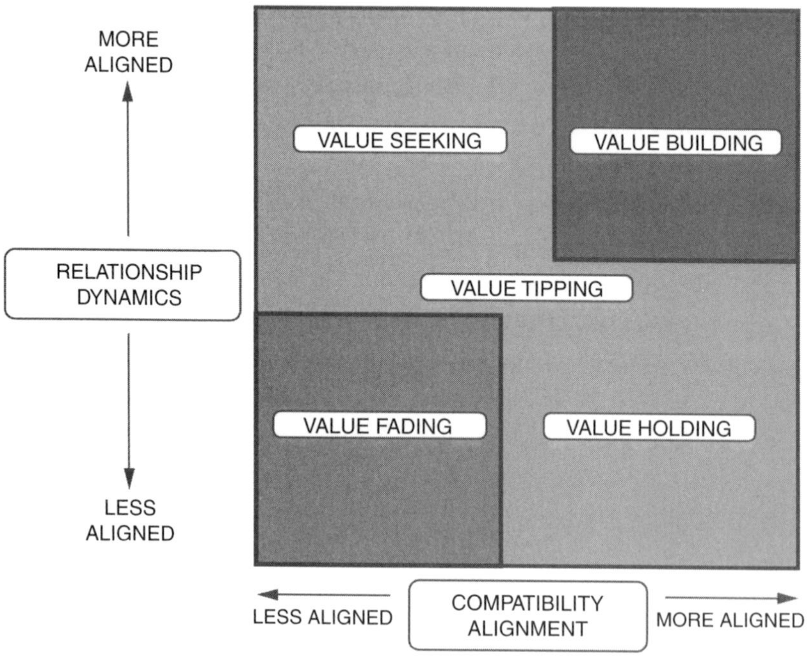

Source: Jerry Ledlow Ph.D. and Karl Manrodt Ph.D. – Used with permission

team orientation, and focus). By plotting individual (and anonymous) responses to the CaT questions on this map, parties have an instantaneous visual representation of the relationship. This map helps companies quickly assess whether their relationship is aligned to build value.

The CaT results are always revealing. Some companies are pleasantly surprised that they are closely aligned. Most agree that the results reflect what most people had been feeling about the relationship for some time but were often unable to verbally communicate.

If partners want to strengthen the relationship and improve performance, something must change. *Change* the people or change the *people*! Unfortunately, some companies learn that they are culturally mismatched. Remember the cultural misfit between the pharmaceutical company and their service provider?

Some cultural misalignment will not by itself prevent parties from creating a highly collaborative business relationship. What can be more damaging is a gap in the parties' perceptions of themselves and each other. People should therefore look for situations where one party has an unjustifiably high opinion of itself or unjustifiably low opinion of its partner. These gaps inhibit trust and can prevent partners from strengthening the relationship. Most compatible relationships have only minor gaps in people's perceptions of themselves and their partners.

For example, in figure 3.3, there are slight gaps in the buying company's own perceptions of its compatibility across all five dimensions and the supplier's perceptions of the buyer. Figure 3.4 depicts an example of high gaps across a buyer and supplier relationship.

When working on developing a highly collaborative relationship, it is important to take these gaps in compatibility and trust seriously. Failure to do so simply delays or derails the teams' efforts at negotiating the relationship.

Recalling the pharmaceutical company and its service provider discussed previously, the companies' CaT scores revealed significant gaps in their self-views and their views of each other. Despite sincere intentions to improve the relationship, there was little compatibility and trust between the companies. Prior to participating in the CaT assessment, the parties were so frustrated that the buying company penalized the service provider by bringing some work in house. Likewise the service provider sued the buying company for breach of contract. The

Figure 3.3  Spider graphic: Low gaps

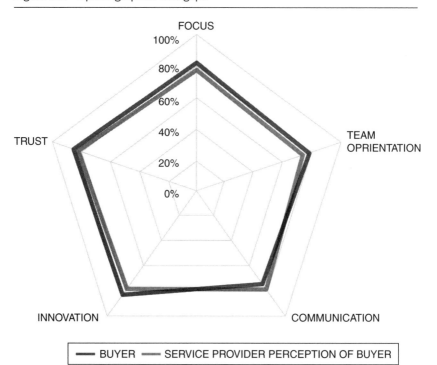

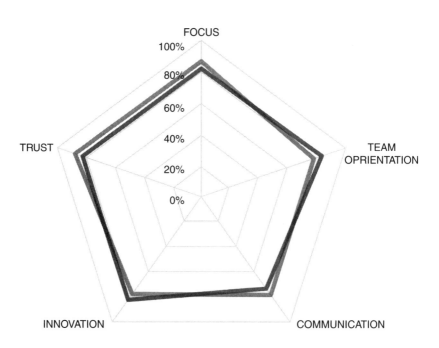

Figure 3.4    Spider graphic: High gaps

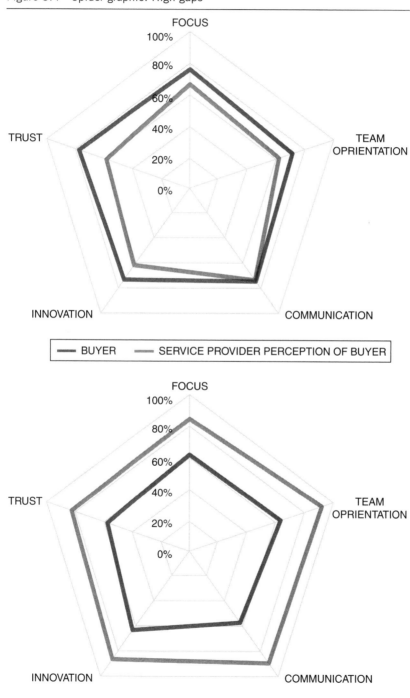

companies subsequently agreed to participate in a CaT assessment, and the results told the true story. The companies were cultural misfits. The increased awareness of a lack of trust and compatibility hit home for each company; the companies agreed they should really never have entered into a business deal in the first place, and they came to the conclusion that the CaT gaps were simply too large to close. They agreed to amicably part ways with the goal to not cause harm to the other party during—and after—the unwinding process.

Naturally, each business should understand its partners, ranging from understanding organizational structure to management style to communication style. Unfortunately, traditional negotiations focus too much on price, and cultural fit is not considered until it is too late—often after the supplier has already started performing the work.

Organizations that want to explore the merits of a WIIFWe mindset should consider building an awareness of their compatibility. This is true regardless of whether they have an existing partnership or are trying to build a new partnership. While the CaT offers a sound tool for assessing compatibility, there are different approaches for determining cultural fit. At the very least, partners should ask the following questions:

- What characteristics do we need from our partners to match our culture?
- How will we evaluate and select for cultural fit?

In a number of external partnering situations, companies provide service providers with "scenarios" as part of the initial selection process. Service providers are invited to describe how they would respond to sample situations. Other companies review a service provider's past behaviors and style attributes (with them and client references) to see whether collaboration and innovation are actually part of the service provider's company culture. Such reviews ought to be a two-way evaluation. Service providers should undertake similar reviews of their current and prospective customers before embarking on the path to We.

Awareness of a cultural mismatch, coupled with an awareness of gaps in perceptions, can encourage companies to become more transparent. Companies must expose the problems in order to improve them. An honest dialogue about what each organization needs to improve the partnership can breathe new life into a stale relationship.

If the new or existing relationship does not have enough trust, transparency, and compatibility, but a more collaborative relationship is desired, begin by working on the gaps across the five dimensions of the CaT with the goal to strengthen the relationship. Without the proper foundation, everyone will face unnecessary challenges.

## The Next Steps

Once the parties believe that the partnership has reached a sufficient level of trust, transparency and compatibility—or if it is willing to work on a new or existing relationship to develop the requisite trust, transparency and compatibility—it's on to the next steps: the rest of this book outlines a clear, practical process for developing a value-creating partnership using a collaborative negotiation style. The next steps are to develop a shared vision and a common set of guiding principles.

# A SHARED VISION AND COMMON GUIDING PRINCIPLES

T he second and third steps in negotiating a relationship create a shared vision and a common set of guiding principles. This is where negotiators begin to realize that the path to We is significantly different from conventional negotiations.

Traditionally, negotiators rarely discuss, much less document, a vision for the relationship or any guiding principles driving collaborative behavior. However, the most successful collaborative relationships do exactly that. Business people and professional negotiators spend time setting the relationship on the right course from the very first conversation by agreeing on the relationship's purpose and behaviors.

This section provides business people and professional negotiators with a clear understanding of the importance of creating a shared vision and a set of common principles that drive collaborative behaviors.

Chapter 4 discusses shared vision statements, with examples of two relationships that have successfully leveraged a shared vision for success. A process for quickly and efficiently reaching a consensus on a shared vision for the journey to We is also outlined.

Chapter 5 details six guiding principles that all highly collaborative relationships should follow to achieve long-term mutual success. The six guiding principles are based on common social norms and help drive collaborative behavior throughout the process of Getting to We from developing a flexible framework for the relationship to relationship management. Because agreement on guiding principles is likely foreign to many readers, sample language that the reader can use as a starting point in the process of Getting to We is provided.

Agreeing on a shared vision and guiding principles is necessary. Skipping these steps could lead to problems later in the process. The vision and the principles must continue to play a dominant role in every aspect of the relationship, provide the needed focus when businesses face challenges, and foster an atmosphere of continuing collaboration.

CHAPTER 4

# STEP 2: CREATING A SHARED VISION

Companies that treat each other as *parties to their success* achieve transformational results because organizations are working together to achieve a shared purpose or vision for the future. Each organization may have different motivations for wanting to achieve that vision, but the vision for the future remains the guiding point. Creating a shared vision may seem out of context for a book on negotiating. Many books that discuss negotiation strategies and tactics recommend that a negotiator's first step is preparation. In the what's-in-it-for-me (WIIFMe) context, this means that a negotiator is simply preparing to maximize his position vis-à-vis his counterpart. Even when approaching a negotiation as a problem-solving exercise, conventional techniques focus on looking through the lens of self-interest to find shared interests as the first step. These cumbersome approaches assume there is no *shared vision* for the future and this is therefore not part of the negotiation.

## WHY A SHARED VISION?

Yogi Berra, the famous baseball player and manager, once quipped that if you don't know where you are going you might not get there.[1] This muddling of words is quite applicable for negotiating successful partnerships. High-performing, highly collaborative partnerships have a purpose that is greater than a series of transactions. Some form to meet an external challenge in the market; others form to perform a core function for a company, and yet others are internally focused to achieve transformational results.

One thing remains constant. The partnerships that have a clearly articulated vision for the future have a much greater chance of reaching their destination. The converse is equally true. Partnerships without a clearly articulated purpose are not as successful as those that have one. Therefore, all highly collaborative partnerships rally behind a shared vision that brings value to the parties.[2]

Creating a shared vision helps parties direct their energy and efforts away from each other to determining the avenue for mutual success. Without a shared vision, businesses and individuals tend to fall victim to a short-term WIIFMe approach as they sit across from each other at the negotiation table.

The process of creating a shared vision gives the parties a reason to stand side by side as they tug on the rope, rather than pulling against each other in a traditional game of tug-of-war. The shared vision not only strengthens the relationship between parties, it can also lead to a deeper understanding of each party's business and how to leverage each other's strengths for mutual gain.

Furthermore, "Visions inspire—*breathe life into*—our work in the here and now, from the most profound to the most mundane,"[3] notes Peter Senge, author of many books on the subject of building effective business teams. Similarly, a shared vision for a partnership breathes life into a We relationship. It gives people in the relationship a bigger purpose.

Still not convinced of the power of creating a shared vision? Let's explore three very real examples of how a shared vision can—or cannot—align and motivate organizations to make a difference in achieving greatness.

## Water For People and Rwanda

Water for People is an international nonprofit development organization on a serious mission. It combines traditional efforts to help people access safe drinking water, such as funding technology, while also using highly collaborative techniques to ensure sustainability, including partnering with individual communities. Its story is noteworthy precisely because Water for People effectively collaborates with communities that have a history of conflict and a history of failed projects founded on good intentions.

Water for People's corporate mission reads as follows:

**Water For People Mission Statement**

Water For People works to build a world where all people have access to safe drinking water and sanitation and where no one suffers or dies from a water—or sanitation—related disease. This is our vision.

We're on a mission. We work with people and partners to develop innovative and long-lasting solutions to the water, sanitation, and hygiene problems in the developing world. We strive to continually improve, to experiment with promising new ideas, and to leverage resources to multiply our impact.[4]

The mission is powerful. But even more powerful is how Water for People uses it to create shared visions with communities, governments, and nongovernmental organizations (NGOs) to provide access to safe drinking water and sanitation.

First, Water for People does not assume that there is a one-size-fits-all vision for the governments and communities it works with. It strives to create unique shared visions with each of them. Then it couples the unique vision statement with specific outcomes so that individual communities can reach their goals of providing sustainable drinking water to their citizens.

Water for People leverages its vision and mission in the approach to partnerships (equivalent to suppliers), some with local villages, some with NGOs, and still others with local entrepreneurs. Water for People currently works in 11 countries around the world.

"Rwanda Challenge,"[5] also known as the Rulindo Challenge, is an example of how Water for People combines its vision and mission with that of a local government to create a unique shared vision that guides how two parties work together to create a lasting impact to not only establish the flow of water in a community, but also to ensure that the solution is sustainable and that fresh water will flow long after Water for People leaves Rwanda.

In 2010, Water for People and the Rwandan government and citizens developed the "Rwanda Challenge" and resulting "Vision 2020" that documents six primary objectives: [6]

**Water for People Rwanda Challenge and Vision 2020**

1.  Meet the United Nations Millennium Development Goal for water and sanitation; ensure environmental sustainability; halve by 2015 the proportion of the population without sustainable access to safe drinking water and basic sanitation;
2.  Ensure the continued implementation of Vision 2020 and the Economic Development and Poverty Reduction Strategy (EDPRS);
3.  Align activities with existing activities of other bodies of the government of Rwanda and other parties;
4.  Bring full coverage in water in the entire district of Rulindo by December 2014, hereby referred to as the "Rulindo Challenge";
5.  Shift from the never-ending community-based projects and the open-ended involvement of international organizations in the country and, instead, show that systematic programming can tackle sustainability challenges, build on existing local capacity and strength, leverage local resources, and serve as a model for future replication;
6.  Accomplish a common work in which strategy, planning, development, monitoring, review, and capacity building are carried out as a joint effort through consultation between the parties of this Memorandum of Understanding.

With the shared vision established, Water for People's country coordinators carefully target county-sized regions to bring them 100 percent water and sanitation coverage. Using their project criteria as well as the strategic planning efforts of the government, Water for People created a collaboration agreement to move ahead in the district of Rulindo, Rwanda.[7]

Water for People is well on its way to success in Rulinda and is expected to achieve its goal by the end of 2014. Rulinda will then join 15 communities of Cuchumuela Bolivia and 14 communities of Chinda, Honduras that have already achieved success.

In every highly successful relationship the authors have studied, the relationship not only had a vision and goals, it aligned individual behaviors and actions to achieve the vision. But nonprofit organizations are not the only organizations that have leveraged individual mission statements into shared vision statements for mutual success with their partners. Most companies have their own form of a mission, vision statement, or charter, but partnerships often lack a joint vision.

Jaguar and Unipart leveraged the power of a shared vision statement to achieve great success.

## Jaguar and Unipart

The Jaguar and Unipart partnership is an excellent example of a shared vision's power to redirect a partnership and achieve mutual success. Jaguar began working with Unipart almost 25 years ago. The initial focus of the outsourcing effort was aftermarket parts fulfillment in the United Kingdom.

When Jaguar entered into its contract with Unipart, Jaguar ranked ninth on customer satisfaction in the J. D. Power and Associates survey. In 1992 Sir Nick Scheele became Jaguar's CEO. Scheele recognized that the relationship was not working as well as it could. He had an informal dinner discussion with Unipart's CEO, John Neill. The goal was to discuss how the companies could improve the business model while also deriving more positive benefits for both Jaguar and Unipart.

These discussions ultimately led to the creation of the following shared vision statement.

> **Jaguar–Unipart Vision Statement**
> To support Jaguar dealers in delivering a Unique Personal Ownership Experience to Jaguar Drivers worldwide, ensuring industry-leading owner loyalty through partnership and world-class logistics.[8]

This shared vision statement embodies a WIIFWe mindset. Not only does the shared vision focus the partnership, it also focuses on the dealerships and Jaguar drivers. This shared vision is also result-oriented and future-focused.

The power behind the shared vision statement is that it aligns Jaguar and Unipart toward one common goal. "Our destinies are linked," explained Neill.[9] Both parties know the purpose of the partnership and use the vision statement to guide them in defining strategic objectives and performance goals.

The shared vision also transcends each company's self-interests. Neill elaborated: "If Jaguar's sales increase, our profits increase, and if their sales go down, we make less money. But we also have the ability to influence sales through the investments we make to innovate and improve our processes."[10]

Finally, Jaguar and Unipart's shared vision is broad and flexible enough to allow the relationship to adjust as circumstances change. As all business professionals know, business is dynamic. A well-crafted shared vision statement keeps the partnership focused on driving business to achieve mutual goals.

The real testament to the success of this vision statement is that it has become embedded in each company's culture, surviving many organizational changes. Neill noted, "There have been personnel changes at Jaguar and Unipart over the years. This sometimes has led to changes in the way we work together, but the shared vision statement helps keep our relationship pointed in the right direction."[11]

The result? The shared vision set the foundation for a WIIFWe mindset, enabling a true collaborative breakthrough between Jaguar and Unipart. The Jaguar and Unipart partnership has led transformational improvements in getting Jaguar's service parts logistics to be best in class and to achieve impressive business results. Less than seven years after penning the shared vision, the duo moved to number 1 in J.D. Power rankings for customer satisfaction in 2010—surpassing Lexus, BMW, and Mercedes Benz. Jaguar has maintained that spot in succeeding years.[12]

## EDD Division of a Large Multinational Company

Not all visions are successful, however. One executive—we'll call her Ann—ran a large division of a multinational corporation. Ann explained that on some projects her division provided critical support to another large division at the same corporation. The other division was known as the EDD division. In essence, her division supplied services in an internal partnership arrangement.

Each year the head of the EDD division would share the over-all EDD vision with each of the divisions that supported EDD. Ann describes the lackluster nature of those annual strategy sessions. "Each year everyone would sit politely and listen. People would nod their heads in agreement with EDD's vision for the year ahead. Then everyone would walk out of that meeting, attend their own division's meetings, and the EDD vision would get set aside. Each division head would create his or her own vision regardless of whether that vision matched the EDD vision.

Ann said, "It's not that we were trying to sabotage EDD. It was more the fact that we had our own priorities and our own metrics for our own departments. When budgets get tight and resources are scarce, we had to choose priorities, and EDD's vision and goals did not make our prior-ity list."[13] The bottom line is, the EDD division had created a vision, but it was certainly not a true shared vision that Ann and the other divisions would willingly commit to support.

Ann's experience pointed to critical flaws in how many companies formulate visions. First, many people create visions by themselves or in a closed loop environment. Not being inclusive and allowing for different perspectives is a missed opportunity to create much needed buy-in. In addition, different perspectives can help expose underlying weaknesses and assumptions and increase the likelihood that the vision can actually be achieved.

Second, some corporate cultures falsely believe that a top-down, dictatorial approach will provide the right motivation to "get people on the bus." People working in such an environment often will not tell their colleagues—let alone management—that they don't believe in the vision. Apathy abounds. Progress is stalled.

Finally, many people think that a positive tone and flashy presen-tation is the same as getting commitment for the vision. Commitment means that people actively support the vision and do what is necessary to help everyone succeed. Many leaders fail to recognize the valuable point that buy-in and commitment are not necessarily the same. One might have buy-in, but for various reasons cannot commit to support the vision. In Ann's case she neither bought into the vision nor was committed to change her priorities to help the EDD division achieve its vision. Her division's priorities and metrics did not align with EDD's.

## Crafting a Shared Vision

Not all relationships need to create a shared vision. Organizations seeking to transform their relationship, their market, to create a competitive advantage, or to introduce a new technology or process together should create shared visions. But simply entering into a basic transactional relationship (such as buying a nonstrategic commodity) likely does not need a shared vision. However, parties in a strategic relationship or thinking about entering into a strategic relationship should take the process of creating a shared vision seriously. The next pages take readers through the key attributes of a shared vision and provide a process to create a shared vision.

Many people worry that establishing a vision statement is too time-consuming, cumbersome, or unnecessary. Visioning sessions are like picking a place to go on vacation. A family could get in the car and just start driving. It doesn't take much time to walk from the front door to the car door. Eventually, that family will get somewhere. Or a family could sit down and decide together how to spend their vacation time, establish a budget, choose the best method for getting there, and what they'll do once they get there. If a family wanted to go on a three-week African Safari, it might take quite a bit of planning and budgeting. Chances are the planned vacations will actually be fun.

High-performing relationships are more like the family planning the safari than the family who gets in the car and just starts driving. Each party wants the equivalent of the exotic vacation and wants to know that the other party is equally committed to that destination.

Many people ask, "What are the key attributes of a shared vision"? There are five important attributes identified as important themes in some of the most successful partnerships.

## Developed Jointly

Ideally, a shared vision statement is jointly developed at the start of a collaborative negotiation process. The parties decide where the partnership is headed and why it is going there. It is a genuine expression of each party's value to the other through the commitment to achieve something that does not yet exist.

## Focused on "We"

A good shared vision focuses on creating a culture and ecosystem where the parties work *together* to ensure mutual success. This is tantamount to considering that a WIIFWe mindset has clear intentions to create value for both parties.

## Focused on the Future and Results

In chapter 2 we discussed the importance of creating a "shadow of the future" to help build trust. A good shared vision describes a future state that is attainable due to the joint efforts of the business relationship. The shared vision statement sets forth the larger, guiding purpose for the business endeavor and for joint collaboration. A good shared vision statement describes what the business will look like at some point in the future.

For example, a consumer electronics manufacturer had a corporate sustainability initiative, but was not meeting its eco-sustainability goals. When creating a shared vision with its facilities management partner, it incorporated the goal of becoming more sustainable into its vision. The vision included an objective to drive sustainability within facilities management to help meet the manufacturer's own long-term sustainability initiatives. But it was not a one-sided vision.

The facilities management company also had initiatives to drive sustainability efforts in the industry. Not only will sustainability help it differentiate itself in a crowded marketplace, the initiatives with the manufacturer will lead to changes and innovative practices that benefit the larger manufacturing community.

## Documented

Partners in highly collaborative relationships take the time and the effort to formally document their purpose. It's not enough to discuss a vision. The vision must be documented.

As Senge says, "People creating together work in different ways. They are anchored in the future rather than in the past, drawn forward by images of what they truly want to see exist in the world. They learn how to work with a distinctive source energy that animates the creative process, the creative tension that exists whenever a genuine vision exists in concert with people telling the truth about what exists now. They learn how to let go of having to have everything worked out in advance and to step forth with boldness into immense uncertainty."[14]

Documenting the shared vision anchors the partnership in a focus on the future and provides continuous guidance from the formation (or reinvigoration) of a business relationship to its day-to-day operations.

## Live the vision

Finally, partners who have developed their shared vision by following the first four attributes for a successful shared vision will now live that vision. One way people live the vision is to recite the vision at the start of all meetings. People at all levels within the relationship from the most senior to the most junior should participate in this ritual. Partners embracing this final attribute find that the vision provides amazing clarity and focus for the conversations that follow.

## SHARED VISION IN PRACTICE

Companies such as Jaguar and Unipart discover that in the process of creating a shared vision their business relationship gets stronger, personal relationships also get better, and it leads to a deeper understanding of each other's business model and how to leverage the other for maximum gain.

The following provides two examples of how a shared vision can be incorporated into a formal agreement or contract:

**Shared Vision Template**

**Option 1**
The parties will work together for the duration of this relationship, in good faith and with the overall mutually desired intention to achieve (*enter the shared vision*). The parties agree that the shared vision will be achieved only by the continuing cooperation, combined mutual efforts, and good relations among and between the

parties and in accordance with the principles as set out in the statement of intent.

**Option 2**
The parties will work together in good faith for the duration of this
relationship to achieve transformational business solutions that are
mutually beneficial to the parties: (*enter the shared vision*) The parties
agree that this shared vision will be achieved only through continuing cooperation, trust, and commitment. In order to achieve the
vision and foster good relations, the parties recognize the importance of adhering to the principles set forth in the statement of
intent.

While this sample provides general guidance, it is helpful to consider
the process that the parties use to form its shared vision statement.

## Collaborative Process

While one party can take the lead, for example, a buying company,
the visioning process is much more than one side foisting its corporate
mission statement on the other. A joint process is a must because the
other party has to buy into the vision in order to achieve extraordinary
results. The story below shows the approach a financial institution and
its service provider took in creating their shared vision.

The process started with the companies recognizing that the relationship was not delivering predicted results. Each party pointed to
the other as the reason for the lackluster results. Shortly before their
agreement was set to expire, they took the Compatibility and Trust
Assessment™ (CaT) discussed in chapters 2 and 3. Not surprisingly,
each party scored the other party low regarding focus (one of the
five elements of the CaT). Neither party knew the shared purpose.
Each was focused solely on a long list of tasks listed in the statement
of work.

The financial institution had a corporate champion who saw
tremendous latent value and wanted to unleash that value for both
companies. The companies wanted to get focused. Each party sent
approximately 15 key stakeholders to an off-site meeting that was

professionally facilitated by a Certified Deal Architect.[15] After some general discussions about their vision, each person in the large group was asked to write down three adjectives that would best describe the future vision for the relationship. For example, the words "innovation" and "cooperation" appeared multiple times. The attendees then went on break while the Certified Deal Architect sorted through the words and created a Pareto chart[16] that provided a simple count of the adjectives. In many cases, different people used the same terms to describe the aspirational nature of the future relationship.

The teams convened from the break into smaller groups of five people each. Each smaller team had members from each company representing different company functions, including finance, operations, and purchasing. Each small team took the most popular words and drafted a vision statement with no more than two sentences. After all five vision statements were written, the statements were distributed for comment. The entire group of thirty picked the two vision statements that best reflected the group's sentiments. From there the Certified Deal Architect used the computer and projector and in real time facilitated the group as they wordsmithed the best parts of each shared vision statement and merged these into one that the entire team could stand behind. Once the group felt good about their edits, someone in the group (not the Certified Deal Architect) recommended the entire group read the shared vision out loud.

The entire process took approximately two and a half hours. After the draft was completed, the Certified Deal Architect asked each team member to anonymously answer in writing two questions: "Do you believe the shared vision is the right direction for our companies?" and "How committed are you to personally supporting the shared vision?" Each person was instructed to write the percentage of agreement with each statement. For example, 100 percent meant the person totally believed the shared vision and the vision provided the right direction for the relationship. The results were astounding. A full 95 percent of the people in the room believed with 100 percent unanimity that the companies were headed in the right direction. And 98 percent of the people in the room were 100 percent committed to going forward.

Once again the Certified Deal Architect summarized the results during a break, and when the group reconvened, individuals had a chance to express any concerns or reservations, with each person asked to provide the biggest obstacles that would prevent the parties from achieving their shared vision.

At the end of the workshop, each party agreed to take the draft vision statement to get buy-in from the "next level down" employees in order to further create buy-in and alignment. Four individuals volunteered to take the feedback and finalize the shared vision that would set the foundation for the future of their relationship.

Following a collaborative process such as the one described above immediately improved the relationship by providing much-needed focus. Here's a checklist to consider in creating a joint shared vision.

## Shared Vision Creation Checklist

- What stakeholders and what functions need to help develop the shared vision?
- Should the meeting be held on-site or off-site?
- Who will facilitate the process? An internal or external resource?
- Will an internal facilitator also need to participate in the vision process as a stakeholder?
- Realistically, how much time can each party dedicate to the process?
- What preparatory work should each stakeholder or team member complete before attending the meeting?
- Who will take the vision and gain buy-in from other team members?

## Effectively Leveraging the Shared Vision

Once the vision is memorialized, the parties will leverage it for success. They should review the shared vision at the start of meetings during the life of the relationship for two reasons. First, as people transition through the relationship, the vision establishes a continuum of purpose. Continuity is often lost as the people who came together to form the relationship move on to other projects or jobs. One such partnership mandated that employees read the vision statement and other portions of their agreement at the beginning of every meeting for the first year of their relationship in order for the vision and principles to take root. Now, as new people enter the relationship, the vision remains a focus for transformational success.

Second, things happen that will impact each company or the business at hand. The vision helps steer a steady course while at the same time addressing business challenges. A company had a fairly good working relationship with its service provider. Senior executives understood the power of the enterprise and drove that message home to the rest of the team. So it was business as usual after the public announcement that one of the parties was about to be acquired.

The shared vision in this case meant that the companies would continue to function throughout the transition. While the vision for the relationship did not change, some of the tasks had to change. At a strategy session shortly after the announcement, the soon-to-be-acquired company's senior executive wrote the vision on the whiteboard for everyone—about 30 people. After reading it aloud, she urged the other executives in the room to discuss the relationship's objectives and tasks in light of the vision *and* the pending acquisition. The bottom line was: they were there to serve the end user regardless of the merger.

There are two main takeaways from this example. The first is that a shared vision statement aligns the companies toward a common goal and also transcends each company's self-interest. The second takeaway is that the shared vision stimulates flexibility and focus. Business is dynamic, so a shared vision statement keeps the parties focused on how to drive the business forward as things change.

Inevitably, an inspirational vision will create tension between what currently exists and what the parties seek in the future. That tension ideally is the source of positive, creative energy. "But creative tension does not by itself produce either anxiety or stress. It is simply the gap between the image of what we truly want to see exist and the world as it is today.... The tension between vision and current reality naturally creates energy for change," Senge says.[17]

Therefore, to effectively manage the tension between the relationship as it exists and what it would like to accomplish in the future, there must be mutual agreement on a set of outcomes or goals. Those shared outcomes are aligned to the vision and establish the incremental steps that the businesses will take to achieve the shared vision for the future.

## WHAT'S NEXT?

You've successfully created a shared vision that is a key component of helping establish a WIIFWe mindset. It's now time to begin the negotiating process to establish the *six essential relationship principles* that will drive collaborative behavior.

# CHAPTER 5

# STEP 3: ESTABLISHING THE SIX ESSENTIAL RELATIONSHIP PRINCIPLES

Cindy Hill wondered, "Is that fair?" Hill, vice president of global sustainability at Jones Lang LaSalle (JLL) and her colleagues at Procter & Gamble (P&G) were wrestling with how to define *fairness* in their relationship.

When P&G outsourced its facilities management to JLL in 2003, one significant P&G property management priority was ecological sustainability. During sustainability discussions, the companies wondered if it was *fair* to hold JLL accountable for results that depended on the cooperation of individual P&G employees. "After all," Hill said, "we can put recycling bins in every corner, but we can't force people to drop in their cans and paper."[1]

This is an example of the kinds of conversations business people have about fairness every day. Companies that embrace the WIIFWe philosophy turn to guiding principles to help them make the right decisions when potential conflicts or questions like the one above occur. Thus it is essential to have agreed upon guiding principles, preferably documented and integrated into the day-to-day social norms that embody the intent and culture of the relationship.

The third step on the path to We is to agree upon a set of guiding principles, telling the parties how to act within the relationship. Chapter 2 discussed the key importance of trust and the necessary steps to build and maintain trust. Being trustworthy means openly declaring how organizations behave toward each other. This means a company tells its counterpart *how* it will behave, not the specifics of what it will do or not do. Each party declares it will act in accordance with a set of guiding principles. When parties mutually agree upon a set of guiding principles, they lay a behavioral foundation for a trusting and productive relationship—provided that they also act in accordance with their expressed intentions. Think of these guiding principles as the cultural norms or values the parties use to guide behaviors with the intention to build a trusting relationship aimed at achieving the shared vision.

Often, people don't take the time to establish guiding principles for their relationship. They believe it takes too much time and think it's not worth the effort. Instead, they focus on what they think is important: the "substance" of the deal, such as a detailed description of what will be delivered, pricing, risk-assignment, and the legal terms and conditions that will contractually bind the parties.

In high-functioning collaborative partnerships the relationship *is* the substance. It is within the relationship that the parties can solve joint business problems as they occur. The relationship is like a ship that carries the parties toward their jointly set visions and goals; to get there they must make the ship strong and stable.

To achieve a WIIFWe mindset everyone involved must make sure that their interactions are fair. But agreeing on a single standard of fairness is impractical and unworkable. Agreeing on a set of principles reduces—if not eliminates—opportunism, leading to a fairer, more balanced and workable decision-making process.

The principles constitute the substance on which the relationship is based.[2] There are six core principles that, together with the principle of trust described in chapter 2, are more important than any other principles in collaborative relationships. The six principles are:

1. Reciprocity
2. Autonomy
3. Honesty
4. Equity
5. Loyalty
6. Integrity

These are principles of *action*, telling the parties how to act and behave in relation to one another when establishing and living the relationship. Parties must jointly commit to follow these principles as their relationship is established and as business happens during the lifetime of the relationship. By recognizing and acting in accordance with these principles in relation to one another, collaborating companies show that they care more for the relationship than for their short-term self-interest. Thus, it is by living by these principles that trust is created and maintained.

Each of these six essential relationship principles is explored in what follows, with the goal to provide enough information and direction to help begin the conversations and to negotiate each principle.

## RECIPROCITY

In a collaborative relationship, the parties must first commit to the principle of reciprocity. Reciprocity obligates them to make fair and balanced exchanges. If one party accepts a business risk, the other must be prepared to do the same. If one party commits to invest time and money in an important project, the other party must be prepared to reciprocate. They decide what is fair and balanced through the negotiation conversation and by applying the rest of the guiding principles.

Many people learn about making fair trades in early childhood. Children are taught that it is important to share toys and to take turns, and some children learn about trade-offs when playing with trading or collectable cards. Many consider reciprocity (making fair trades) the most fundamental social principle. Society cannot thrive without at least a modicum of unity, and unity will not form and endure without reciprocity. This social principle applies equally to business relationships.

A truly collaborative business relationship is built on a strong foundation of reciprocity. Why? Without reciprocity there is no win-win situation. Reciprocity ensures a fair allocation of obligations, risks, and rewards. One company may take on additional obligations and in turn is rewarded by its partner. Or one company does a small favor for the other, such as extending an important deadline, and is in turn rewarded in kind. Therefore making fair trades is the cornerstone to a mutually beneficial agreement.

Fair and balanced exchanges build trust, and trust is the foundation of all successful relationships. When business people choose to make fair trades, they are trustworthy.

## Reciprocity in Practice

In the P&G and JLL outsourcing agreement, JLL was not in charge of P&G's Clairol properties. Early in the relationship, an incident affecting production occurred at one of the Clairol properties. Within hours of the incident, JLL personnel were on-site to complete an assessment and develop an action plan in an effort to get the Clairol property back to full operating status as quickly as possible. "That level of initiative and cooperation earned credibility and trust for the partnership. We wanted a supplier that would step up, take initiative, and not say 'it's not in the contract'—and JLL was doing just that," explained William Reeves, at the time P&G's corporate real estate leader.[3]

JLL did what was right for the relationship, but it was not in the contract. It was a bold move because there were no formal promises that "out-of-scope" work would be compensated.

JLL responded to the incident the way P&G and JLL initially intended. Both parties were trustworthy to fulfil their intentions. P&G's true testament of reciprocity occurred when they awarded JLL with a five year early renewal of their contract.

## Two Forms of Reciprocity

The principle of reciprocity has been subject to extensive research. Chapter 1 describes Robert Axelrod's research in which game theorists played computerized iterations of the Prisoner's Dilemma.[4] Axelrod learned that the best cooperative strategy is "tit-for-tat."[5] Tit-for-tat is best described as a strategy of one party mirroring the response of the other party. As long as one party cooperates, the other party will likely cooperate. However, when one party defects, the other party likely will defect. Thus, reciprocity obliges the parties to return favors granted, gifts given, and concessions made, thereby creating more value through cooperation than through noncooperation.

Most people don't take the time to distinguish between two forms of reciprocity when negotiating—short-term and long-term reciprocity. When two people make an *immediate* exchange of value, they are making a trade-off or triggering a short-term obligation of reciprocity. For example, a buying company could increase a service provider's scope of work in exchange for a reduction in price on all of the work the service provider performs. On the other hand, when one person gives something up with the hope of reciprocity at some future time, that person is triggering a long-term obligation of reciprocity. If a supplier fulfills an expedited shipment at no additional cost to the customer (but at an internal cost to the supplier), the supplier hopes that the customer will remember this act of kindness at some point in the future. But what if the customer doesn't? Resentments will grow since the principle of reciprocity—so powerful in every society—has been violated.

Concessions can be a form of long-term reciprocity when the other company eventually acts in kind and puts the relationship back in balance. For example, a supplier solving a pending crisis without being formally obliged to under the contract is not making a concession, rather it is acting under the principle of reciprocity, expecting something in return at some other time.

Most negotiators feel comfortable when they are vague about whether the concession they are demanding will be returned at some point in time. Some business people simply don't know if, when, or how their company will make the exchange fair and balanced at some point in the future. Other negotiators demand unilateral concessions to drive down pricing and never intend to make the exchange fair and balanced.

## Expressing Intentions about Reciprocity

While people may believe they understand the principle of reciprocity, it is necessary to discuss and define the obligations involved. By doing so, each party is making a commitment to the other to act in accordance with the principle and write down the intention for future reference.

Here are some topics for discussion to help the relationship define reciprocity:

**Topics to Define Reciprocity**

- For established relationships, have each party give an example of successful long-term reciprocity within the relationship. Explain why the obligation of reciprocity was triggered and what the receiving party did to reciprocate.
- For new relationships, give an example of successful long-term reciprocity from another relationship. Explain why the obligation of reciprocity was triggered and what the giving party knows of the receiving party's efforts to reciprocate.
- Describe a way in which you or your company was disappointed when you or your company did something that did not trigger any reciprocity.
- What obstacles might each party face when being asked to reciprocate (for instance, corporate policy against any promise of future action)?

The answers will help the parties define reciprocity for the relationship. One party is not imposing its ideas on the other. Rather, by discussing the answers to these questions, each looks for common themes, words, or feelings and then uses these to craft a statement of intention regarding reciprocity. For example, a statement of intent regarding reciprocity might read like this:

**Suggested Statement of Intent: Reciprocity**

*In keeping with the obligation of reciprocity, we will strive to make exchanges, whether large or small, that are mutually beneficial to the parties. We will not make any demand upon the other that we ourselves are not willing to return in kind. We recognize that reciprocity lies at the heart of this relationship's ability to reach its goals and will ensure that all short-term and long-term requests are for the mutual benefit of each party and the relationship.*

The theme of mutual benefit is the cornerstone of this statement of intent. However, the relationship may have other ways to express reciprocity. The idea is to document the intention early on the path to We.

Each party will rely heavily on this statement of intent when negotiating other elements of the relationship such as an exchange of monetary value and the governance process.

## AUTONOMY

In a collaborative relationship, the parties must commit to the principle of autonomy, which means abstaining from using power to promote one party's sef-interest at the expense of the other. The specific meaning of autonomy is debated among philosophers, political thinkers, and social scientists. But all agree that autonomy is important in creating a positive work environment. Mihály Csíkszentmihályi[6] (in *Flow: The Psychology of Optimal Experience*), Malcolm Gladwell[7] (in *Outliers: The Story of Success*), and Daniel Pink[8] (in *Drive: The Surprising Truth About What Motivates Us*) have focused on the importance of autonomy in their popular books. At the individual level, autonomy refers to the ability to act based on reasons and motives reflecting the individual's own values and convictions. The same applies to business relationships. People want to make their own decisions, free from the power of another; they want to work as equals and they want to be part of a process that allows them to make decisions in sync with the group.

The infamous specter of bargaining power usually casts a shadow over commercial relationships. A company holding a strong position instinctively tends to use it to gain short-term benefits, while the company in the weaker position struggles to improve its BATNA (the best alternative to a negotiated agreement) to escape the other party's grip.

Power struggles can come in many forms. Good examples include demanding unilateral concessions, hiding known risks, shifting known risks to the other party, or micro-management. These types of power plays disrupt a company's ability to make rational decisions that are in its best interest *and* in the interest of the relationship.

Experience and economic theory show that the usual strategy to use one's power is flawed. Instead of trying to force their will upon each another, the parties should abide by the principle of autonomy: giving room for independent decision-making by each party.

A relationship characterized by autonomy has several benefits. Autonomy leads to greater innovation, which ultimately can lead to competitive advantages. Autonomy acts as a "facilitator" by allowing the parties to live the other core principles, such as reciprocity, honesty, and loyalty—for why should anyone be honest and loyal to another who forces their will upon them? In turn, those principles lead to more creative problem-solving and innovation. And autonomy, like all of the principles, strengthens trust. When a stronger party chooses not to use its power, it shows trust that the other party still will act in the former's interests.

## Autonomy in Practice

In 1952 the US Atomic Energy Commission established a highly secret site outside of Denver to fabricate triggers that contained plutonium and uranium fuel for nuclear weapons. By 1989, the site had become one of the most dangerously contaminated locations in the world. The US Environmental Protection Agency (EPA) designated the Rocky Flats plant and surrounding 6,262-acre site as a hazardous waste site, and President George H.W. Bush eventually ordered the site permanently closed and cleaned up.

Multiple government units had some jurisdiction over the Rocky Flats Closure Project. After years of discord, they came together in 1996 and agreed to the provisions contained in the Final Rocky Flats Cleanup Agreement (FRFCA).

The FRFCA agreement established the regulatory framework for achieving the ultimate cleanup of the site and defined the vision that broke with traditional standards to ensure a decision-making process that allowed the joint venture between Kaiser Engineers and CH2M Hill (Kaiser-Hill) some autonomy in making decisions that met the FRFCA's vision and goals.

For example, Kaiser-Hill and the US Department of Energy (DOE) had broadly outlined the fundamental tenets for the cleanup project and left much of the decision-making process to Kaiser-Hill. Kaiser-Hill employees and subcontractors were encouraged to think outside of the box. One Kaiser-Hill employee commented, "Workers were encouraged to question the status quo. If a task was typically done in a certain way, the workers would talk about whether that task needed to be done differently. Independent decision making led to cleanup techniques never before conceived of."[9] For example, when faced with a project to dismantle a building, Kaiser-Hill would approach the tasks associated with dismantling the building without the micromanagement associated with many buyer/supplier relationships.

It may seem paradoxical that the principle of autonomy, essentially a principle of independence, is of crucial importance for commercial relationships in which the parties obviously become highly dependent. Some may also say that this principle is in conflict with the principle of loyalty to the relationship (which is discussed below). The opposite is in fact true. Only autonomous parties can form a truly collaborative business relationship in the first place.

## Autonomy's Two Aspects

There are two aspects to the principle of autonomy:

- The parties work together as equals despite the possibility that one may have more power than the other.
- Each party is allowed to make decisions without any coercion from the other.

Many business relationships begin as two or more independent companies with an unbalanced distribution of power and without an adequate governing process in place. The more powerful party uses its power to get its way, sometimes affecting the decision-making process of the weaker party. That then triggers a series of reactions and counterreactions—a game of continuous defections, the opposite of the collaborative game of tit for tat.

It's intriguing that a lack of autonomy seems—well, so normal in many relationships. It feels strange not to use power for an immediate benefit when the chance presents itself. An executive once said as he stood in front of a representative of his company's service provider, "Listen, if the CFO comes to me and tells me to take $1 million out of the bottom line, then I'm going to look at him [the service provider] and tell him to take $1 million out of his costs to us. That's the way it's going to work."[10] He was reminded that this was the way it used to work. When the principle of autonomy was explained to this executive, his counterpart at the service provider chimed in that if given the opportunity to tackle a problem and with the ability to look at all the options for reducing spending, he could easily take $1 million out of the bottom line costs, just not in the way initially conceived.

Companies that use and abuse power to dictate solutions will get less than optimal solutions. In their show of power they express hubris since they force their will upon the weaker party. They deny that the weaker party may have much better ideas, knowledge, and solutions regarding a particular problem. With the principle of autonomy in place, however, people are free to bring the best of their problem-solving skills to the table. And more important, when people are free to act in the relationship's best interests, they will.

The executive mentioned above was impressed with the response from his counterpart: "Well, if you can do that [solve my problem], I'm all in."[11] Because high-performing relationships are based on principles, the right thing to do is to rely on those principles to guide the parties through the appropriate governance procedure to jointly resolve a problem. Companies simply cannot throw their weight around and still have a high-performing relationship.

Let's explore each of the two aspects of autonomy in more detail.

### Work as Equals

There's a joke that elicits nervous laughter from service providers: "The Golden Rule in business is that he who has the gold, rules." This simple joke reflects the traditional power imbalance in most business relationships where the buying company tends to have more power than the service provider. However, it is important to remember that service providers can also hold a power imbalance when they dominate a market with little competition.

In a relationship the parties are autonomous when the obligations and responsibilities of the relationship are viewed by everyone involved as legitimate. In other words, demands are based on valid principles, reasons, and arguments from everyone's perspective. This further means that, under the principle of autonomy, the only power the parties may use when negotiating or governing the relationship is the power of the best argument. Autonomous parties must always be ready to answer questions such as, "Why do you think that proposal is valid?" Or, "How does that follow from the spirit of our relationship?" And "Why is that fair?" If there are no valid answers, the proposal must be altered and adapted to conform to legitimate principles.

Furthermore, working as equals means that people are allowed to do what they do best despite the fact that one may have more power than the other, especially economic power. Businesses choose to partner because they each see the value in what the other brings to the table. If this were not the case, the businesses would not work together or only do so at a minimal level.

For this reason, parties should focus on *what* needs to be accomplished, not on *how* it will be accomplished. Therefore, they must define outcomes so that the businesses doing the actual work or providing the service can determine the best way to achieve those outcomes.

### Independent Decisions Free From Coercion

A truly collaborative relationship is free from coercion. Coercion is based on power, which always arises when parties perceive that one of the parties is more dependent on the other party than vice versa. For example, if we are more dependent on you than you are on us, you have power over our actions. If we want to sell a company, you may be the only realistic buyer for us. The buyer, however, may have several options. Thus, we are more dependent on the buyer than you are on us, which gives you the power to influence our decisions.

The force of coercion is felt most clearly in contract negotiations. Coercion can come in many forms, and at the bargaining table it is usually a threat of some sort, such as telling an incumbent supplier that the company will move the business to the supplier's competitor if the supplier doesn't reduce its prices. Succumbing to the threat is against the supplier's interests, but it appears better than the alternative: losing the customer's business.

Ironically, even when bargaining power is used to get what is wanted in the contract, there is an inclination to deny that coercive power is being used. Parties don't want to admit that they are using a stronger bargaining position to achieve lopsided goals. In fact, this inclination is the principle of autonomy working internally, because this principle obliges a party not to use the power it holds.

For example, at a cocktail party, one senior sales executive believed that his company's near monopoly in the market did not give his company an advantage over its customers. In the face of some polite disagreement, the executive justified his company's power by saying it was only fair that his company got what it asked for, suggesting that its suppliers could choose to not work with his company. After all, it's a free market, right?

The use (and abuse) of power, however, creates a huge roadblock on the path to We. Intuitively, it is understood that reciprocity will create a genuine collaborative relationship *only* if the parties can exercise free will—uninfluenced by the bargaining power of the other party. And when reciprocity is undermined, so is trust.

Using bargaining power comes at a cost precisely because the weaker party will defend itself. As in the tit-for-tat game, companies respond in kind to what their counterpart does. As soon as the weaker party retaliates, the stronger party will do likewise. And on it will go until something drastically changes.

One way that parties free themselves from coercive power is by allowing everyone an equal seat at the table to develop the terms of the relationship. How companies choose to address relationship provisions is a key indicator of their commitment to We. Organizations seeking to impose rules and procedures without extensive dialogue and explanation are highly unlikely to have a WIIFWe mindset when the going gets tough.

## Expressing Intentions about Autonomy

Autonomy is a completely new concept in many business relationships. Companies must take the time to understand this principle and must allow each company in a relationship to make decisions free from any form of coercion.

Here are some topics for discussion to help understand and define autonomy:

---

**Topics to Define and Understand Autonomy**

- How do you each (customer and supplier) experience pressure to make decisions that are not in your company's best interest? What are the ramifications?
- How does your company tend to make decisions? (Describe the process, the information people like to have, the time frame for authorization).

- For established relationships, have each party describe a situation in which it received enough information to make an informed decision about something important.
- For new relationships, have each party describe a situation in which it received enough information to make an informed decision about something important.
- What does "working as equals" mean for this endeavor? (Be specific because this concept will not be the same for every relationship.)
- In what ways might any real or perceived power imbalance conflict with an intention to work as equals as the parties define it? How will they work with those conflicts?

The answers will help the parties understand autonomy in regard to their relationship. Not all business relationships will define autonomy in the same way, yet having one definition that all can live by is critical for success. This discussion ideally would center on common themes, words, or feelings. These common themes and words would then go into a statement of intention regarding autonomy. For example, a statement of intent regarding autonomy might read like this:

**Suggested Statement of Intent: Autonomy**

*In keeping with the obligation of autonomy, neither party will seek to use its power to wrongfully induce the other to make a decision that is against its best interests and those of the relationship. We will strive to make as much information available as possible to allow our partner to make good decisions for itself and for the relationship.*

*Further, we seek to work as equals in all of our interactions. We define working as equals as [insert definition here]. We recognize that working as equals and being free from coercion ensures our ability to reach our own goals and those of the relationship.*

The themes of working as equals, as defined by the parties, and freedom from coercion are the cornerstones of this statement of intent.

However, a relationship may have other ways to express autonomy and should include those concepts in this statement of intent. The idea is to document the intention early on the path to the We mindset. Each party will rely heavily on this statement of intent throughout the life of the relationship.

## HONESTY

Parents tell their children that honesty is the best policy. How often have you witnessed people (individuals or companies) bury their head in the sand instead of confronting brutal facts? The application of honesty as the best policy can often get lost in the business world. This is especially true when individuals can hide behind the curtain of a business where the largest impact of risk is borne by the company.

In a collaborative relationship, the parties *must* commit to the principle of honesty. Fundamentally, honesty obliges the parties to tell the truth, both about facts in the world and about their intentions and experiences.

While the virtues of honesty have been espoused since the beginning of mankind, Dan Ariely[12] has put the importance of honesty in business relationships front and center in his research and popular books. Ariely is a professor of psychology and behavioral economics at Duke University and is the founder of the Center for Advanced Hindsight. He has authored multiple books on the topic, and his most recent *The (Honest) Truth About Dishonesty: How We Lie to Everyone— Especially Ourselves*[13] is especially thought-provoking.

Ariely encourages individuals and organizations to call out dishonesty immediately. It's not just the impact of the transgression—but the impact that can happen when dishonesty becomes a social norm in day-to-day business practices. Ariely points out that cheating can become contagious and that group dynamics and behavior can have a powerful effect on each individual. He calls this "wishful blindness" and explores the concept as it relates to the Enron collapse in 2001.

In his examination of the Enron accounting scandal, Ariely writes that one consultant working for Enron while the company was rapidly disintegrating "said he hadn't seen anything sinister going on. In fact, he had fully bought into the worldview that Enron was an innovative leader of the new economy right up until the moment the story was all over the headlines."[14]

More surprisingly, once the story of Enron's corruption broke, the consultant "could not believe that he failed to see the signs all along." How often have we found ourselves in that kind of situation, with wishful blindness preventing us from facing the facts? We have witnessed what Ariely is talking about—seeing people in business relationships who think they are behaving honestly and fairly when they really aren't. Simply put, they can't see the forest for the trees. That's why Ariely points out that people need to "figure out ways to contain and control" perverse urges and activities that can destroy business relationships.[15]

Honesty can have a big impact on a company's willingness to be transparent. Many business people ask, "If I am open and honest with them, are the other guys being open and honest with me? How will I know?" Experiences with opportunism can produce fears that a dishonest party will take advantage of honest discourse by using information against the honest one. This in turn drives further opportunism. The argument goes something like this: "I don't think that she is being honest with me, so I'll withhold a little information. It isn't all that important so it's no big deal." Except that the other party is thinking and doing the same thing. Both have justified dishonesty.

Being honest builds trust and without trust companies cannot break through WIIFMe thinking. Being honest includes opening up about vulnerabilities. In order to really build trust, companies have to be honest about things that others can potentially use to their advantage. By being honest, they are both trustworthy and trusting with each other.

## Honesty (and Dishonesty) in Practice

In their original 2003 agreement, JLL did not perform real estate transaction work for Procter & Gamble. JLL had done an excellent job for P&G under its existing contract, and it hoped to expand its business in this area with P&G. When JLL approached P&G about taking on the real estate portion of the business, P&G was brutally honest: "We love your service—and we think you'd do great in Asia and Europe. But you don't meet our standards in the United States, and we will need to competitively bid this work." Of course, JLL was deeply disappointed. Yet, this level of honesty spurred JLL to reexamine the vulnerability of its operations and make strategic investments to improve their capabilities. In 2008, JLL won the work under a competitive bidding process.[16]

Lauralee Martin, JLL's chief executive officer of the Americas (formerly chief operating officer/chief financial officer) explained, "It's important to our future success that companies like P&G can feel good about having these transparent and fact-based discussions. In the end, it makes us a stronger and more viable provider not only for P&G, but for all of our clients."[17]

This story says something about the benefits of honesty. Examples of how a lack of honesty can damage relationships are abundant. A boutique consulting firm worked with a wide array of clients, many of whom needed specialized help. The consulting firm would reach out to a community of experts to join the team for the purpose of meeting a particular client's needs. This interrelated web of relationships worked as long as people acted with integrity.

A consultant agreed to accept an assignment with the boutique firm and then dropped out of the assignment, citing various reasons. The firm soon realized that the consultant had been offered more lucrative work by another firm. When the firm called to discuss the situation with the consultant, he claimed financial hardship and that the circumstance was a one-time event. The consultant promised to be committed to the firm and its clients in all future engagements.

For a time, the consultant and the firm worked well together. The consultant was appreciative of the firm's commitment to him by giving him a second chance. Yet, as soon as a more lucrative consulting assignment came along, the consultant once again left to work on the financially more lucrative project.

After some time the consultant called the firm to find out why he had not been assigned to any more client work. The firm's managing director told the consultant that he did not act with honesty and was untrustworthy and unreliable. There would be no further assignments. What could have been a beautiful relationship was destroyed because of the lack of honesty.

## Honesty's Two Aspects

Healthy relationships require honesty as the only policy. But what exactly does honesty mean? The themes of accuracy and authenticity are the cornerstones of honesty.

### *Accuracy*

Accurate or fact-based conversations separate the facts from the explanations that interpret or color those facts.[18] A fact is something that is observable. An explanation accounts for the fact. For example, a woman walks up to another woman in a crowded room and whispers something in another woman's ear. An insecure person might think the speaker is gossiping about someone in the room, divulging information that she should not be divulging, or is rude for speaking in front of people who are not supposed to hear that information. A secure person would likely notice the observable facts—one woman talking in a whisper to another woman—and think one woman had something private to say to the other woman. Each of these explanations casts the conversation in a particular light.

Similarly, relationships with a history of conflict, micromanagement, or unfulfilled promises tend to talk less about the observable facts—one woman said something to another woman in a whisper—and more about the perception of those facts; your teammates spend a lot of time gossiping about one another, for example.

Because honesty means telling the truth about external, observable facts and about internal experiences regarding the facts, parties should be careful to separate the two. They can observe some facts and have a perception about those facts; the facts remain constant but the perception does not.

For example, a very large aerospace manufacturer had two divisions working together to make a system for commercial jets. Several years ago a customer complained that the same component contained in three of the last systems was defective and demanded to know what the aerospace manufacturer was going to do about it.

The aerospace manufacturer called a meeting comprising quality control individuals from two separate divisions. Division A represented specific parts within the system, while division B represented parts from the rest of the system and had the relationship with the customer. The

observable facts were that the customer complained that the same component contained within three systems was defective. The explanations
of those facts could be very different from each point of view—the customer, the supplier as one company, and each division.

Conflict and potentially dishonest conversations arise when the
teams meet and *talk as if the explanations of the facts were the facts themselves.*
Initially, the conversations between division A and B were contentious
and filled with blame. Each division was sure that the other division
was responsible for the component's defects. Division B accused division A of having poor quality control measures, while division A accused
division B of rushing the production process and thus damaging system components. This conversation began to spiral out of control and
became destructive rather than productive.

"An accurate conversation starts with mutually observable facts
and finishes with a valuable explanation," explain Connolly and
Rianoshek in *Communications Catalyst.*[19] A valuable explanation is one
in which all stakeholders see value in the explanation of the facts.
To have a valuable conversation each person starts by discussing the
observable facts and claiming the explanation as his or her *perception
of the facts* and not as a fact. Once the quality control people started
talking about observable facts, and not about the explanation, several people began to wonder if the customer was installing the component improperly. The conversation shifted from people being
committed to their explanation about the customer's complaints to
being committed to finding a solution to the customer's complaints.

Further investigation revealed that the same group of employees at the customer's plant were incorrectly installing the "defective"
component. There was nothing wrong with the component at all. The
aerospace manufacturer sent a team of people to train the customer's
employees on the proper way to install the component.

This situation demonstrates the need to discuss facts as separate
from people's perception of the facts as components of telling the truth.
It was not true that the system was defective or that one division was to
blame. Yet *initially,* the customer and both divisions talked about the
explanation for the facts as if their version of the facts were the truth!

In some relationships, even agreeing on one set of observable facts
can be difficult. Unfortunately, many companies do not engage in joint

reporting efforts. Often one party is the keeper of the facts in terms of reporting and analysis. For example, a service provider struggled with having accurate, fact-based conversations because it could not even agree on the facts with the customer. The customer prepared all the reports used for grading the service provider and for determining whether the service provider received its portion of the management fee that was "at risk" (an incentive/penalty fee). The service provider never accepted the customer's facts even though the customer claimed that numbers don't lie. Conversations became so contentious that some team members were barely on speaking terms.

Senior leadership at the companies initiated joint reporting efforts for scoring the service provider. As soon as the reporting efforts became a joint effort to portray observable facts, conversations quickly became more honest and productive because the companies could trust that the data was accurate.

*Authenticity*

Authentic conversations take accurate conversations to the next level of value to all the stakeholders. Authentic conversations start as accurate conversations and then leverage multiple points of view to gain new insights and opportunities for improvement, growth, or change.[20] When conversations are authentic, each person's point of view is genuine while that person also recognizes that an individual point of view is not the whole story. "Authenticity assumes that there is more truth at the intersection of relevant facts, your view, and mine than in either of those three alone."[21]

Personal observations, experiences, and perceptions are important as long as they remain one person's observations, experiences, and perceptions among those of many others. No person's set of observations, experiences, and perceptions should be considered as true unless everyone in the conversation agrees that that person's point of view is the valuable explanation for all stakeholders.

Interestingly, this aspect of honesty always gets the most attention from people. When a dialogue is opened about authenticity, some pushback will often occur. People are uncomfortable with discussing the meaning and purpose of authenticity in the relationship. Some believe that authenticity in the workplace is often interpreted as vulnerability. People fear opening themselves up for criticism if their experience of a situation differs from that of others. Some people dismiss diverging points of view on the same set of facts, believing the divergent views are illegitimate and not worthy of consideration.

Connolly and Rianoshek observe, "Authentic conversations have a distinct character. They value inclusion over exclusion, curiosity over prejudice, commonality over difference, and inquiry over domination."[22] Authentic conversations look to the larger system of relationships in order to achieve the relationship's vision and goals.

Ideally, honest conversations are both accurate and authentic and constantly looking to add value for all stakeholders. When there is any chance that a conversation could be clouded by perceptions masquerading as facts and/or any opportunity to seek a larger truth for the benefit of the relationship, those involved should answer the following questions in this order. (In some situations it will be helpful to have a facilitator who has nothing at stake to guide the conversation and keep it on track.)

---

**Understanding Accuracy and Authenticity**

**Accuracy**
- What are the facts each person at the meeting see in the situation?
- What are the common observable facts all can agree on?
- What are people's perceptions, observations, or explanations of the common, observable facts?
- What explanation for the facts brings value to all stakeholders (including the end user and stakeholders)?

**Authenticity**
- What can you (we) learn from each person's point of view, perception, and/or explanation of the facts?
- What opportunities does a combined point of view uncover?
- What is the big picture as a result of looking for the intersection of all points of view?

---

These questions will help the discussion stay on track, producing a high-value and honest solution to any problem.

## Expressing Intent about Honesty

Obviously, honesty is not a new concept to many business relationships, but defining accuracy and authenticity for the relationship is new. Parties that acknowledge the importance of accurate and authentic conversations have seen improved outcomes, as bickering, pettiness, and open conflict diminish.

Here are some discussion topics to help each party understand and define honesty from the perspective of accuracy and authenticity:

**Topics to Define and Understand Honesty**

- Where do we as a relationship have accuracy in the form of common observable facts and joint reporting?
- Where do we as a relationship confuse an explanation of a fact with the fact(s) itself?
- What situations prompt a more authentic response (a response that looks to the larger value for all stakeholders from accepting all points of view on a set of facts)?
- What situations prompt a less authentic response?
- How can the relationship (the vision and goals) be served by having accurate and authentic conversations?

Answering the questions will help companies understand how to become more accurate and authentic. Again, as people from each company participate in this conversation, look for common themes, words, or feelings. These common themes and words would then go into a statement of intention regarding honesty. For example, a statement of intent regarding honesty might read like this:

**Suggested Statement of Intent: Honesty**

*In keeping with the obligation of honesty, we will strive to have accurate and authentic conversations at all levels within the relationship. We will choose joint (but not duplicate) reporting whenever feasible to encourage "one version of the truth." We will also choose to separate the facts from people's observations, perceptions, and experiences of the facts, and we will speak to our own perception of the facts. We will then look for the greater good that can come from accepting all points of view as relevant for seeking greater value for all stakeholders.*

## LOYALTY

"Trust brings loyalty. Loyalty brings extra effort. Extra effort brings innovation and other results to the bottom line," said Michael Boccio, OSI Group's vice president and McDonald's North American Business Team Lead.[23]

Because McDonald's and the suppliers are loyal to its System, suppliers that have helped McDonald's succeed have themselves likewise achieved success by building their own business in ways they hadn't thought possible. Cryogenic freezing methods are one example. Quickly freezing meat patties has helped the entire foodservice industry, but it was McDonald's that benefited first from the innovation because McDonald's and its suppliers are loyal to the System.

Reciprocity, autonomy, and honesty are not enough to embody a WIIFWe mindset. The parties in a collaborative relationship must also commit to the principle of loyalty. Loyalty is chosen as a principle because it obliges the parties to be loyal *to the relationship*. Loyalty to the relationship—or "System first" thinking as McDonald's calls it—will come when the parties' interests are treated as equally important.

To get to We the parties must view the relationship as its own entity with its own set of interests, such as lowering costs, supporting innovation, and promoting growth. Loyalty is *not* being loyal under all circumstances to one of the parties. It is not about sticking together no matter what. Loyalty is about loyalty *to the relationship as a single entity.*

Many companies struggle with loyalty to the relationship, and some may need to change their corporate culture. This kind of loyalty runs counter to an instinctive need to stay vigilant and protected. Corporate buying practices such as those that encourage frequent bidding for supplies and services are designed to protect the buying company from service providers that become complacent on cost or performance. The reasoning is twofold. First, buyers want to drive down costs, so they bid the work frequently to capture the least expensive pricing for that piece of work. Second, service providers can become too embedded with the buying company, thus exposing it to risks, such as an inability to shift work away from a company performing poorly. However, constant bidding sends a message that what matters is not loyalty to the relationship but only to the costs of one of the parties, the buyer. The buyer does not treat the service provider's interests as being of equal importance with its own interests. If correctly applied by the parties, the principle of loyalty will keep the costs low for all and the quality of the service provider's services high to the benefit of each party.

Loyalty to the relationship is a completely different way of staying vigilant. High-performing relationships require loyalty to achieve ambitious goals. With the right performance objectives and governance process in place, companies will avoid disruptions at the hands of a supplier performing poorly. Rather than being vigilant and incurring transaction costs through rebidding and transitioning work, We relationships will see to it that costs are contained and performance objectives are met consistently.

For example, one company has experienced both worlds: traditional WIIFMe thinking and the WIIFWe thinking of McDonald's System. "Outside of McDonald's, most of the suppliers are typically in a short-term, win-lose environment that is typically cutthroat, trying to win the next big RFP [request for proposal] or purchase order," said Eric Johnson, owner of Baldwin-Richardson Foods. "At McDonald's, I found myself sitting at the same table and engaging in discussions about how we could all partner to make real impacts for the (McDonald's) System. No other customer I had ever dealt with was even close to this kind of collaboration." Loyalty to the System pays dividends for McDonald's, its franchisees, its customers, and its stakeholders.

## Three Aspects of Loyalty

The principle of loyalty is used to allocate risk and rewards, burdens and benefits between the parties while always keeping focus on what is best for the relationship as a separate entity. To be loyal to the relationship is to do what's in its interest, for example, maximizing revenues and minimizing costs. Again, it is not sticking with the party under all circumstances. It is important to emphasize, however, that a revenue-maximizing solution will not be in line with the principles of loyalty if only one party gains while the other loses, because the party that gained did not treat the party that lost with equal concern for its interests.

There are three main aspects of loyalty to the relationship presented here: appropriate allocation of risk and workload, a relationship that has its own interests, and elimination of information asymmetries.

### Appropriate Allocation of Risks and Workload

An important part of every relationship is risk allocation or deciding who bears the cost if something unexpected happens. Traditionally, each party wants to allocate as much risk as possible to the other party, regardless of who can best mitigate the risks. This approach will increase the costs of the relationship. A company unable to mitigate risks will compensate for the potential risk by adding a "risk premium" to the overall costs of the project. Yet if the risk, let's say a natural disaster, does not occur, the project costs are not reduced. The principle of loyalty obliges the parties to allocate risks to the party able to eliminate the risk or, if that is not possible, to the party best able to manage and mitigate the risk in the most cost-effective manner.

In 2006, Microsoft began a complete restructuring of its major global finance processes and operations. Called the OneFinance initiative, the effort outsourced back-office finance transactions spread across 95 countries to Accenture, a global management consulting, technology services, and outsourcing company. Microsoft and Accenture entered the relationship with the goal to transform Microsoft's entire back-office finance processes, including AP, expense reports and invoices, the requisition to purchase order process, and general accounting.[24]

OneFinance is an example of appropriate risk allocation. When the deal between Microsoft and Accenture was originally inked, Accenture managed currency fluctuations for BPO operations that spanned nearly 100 countries. While Accenture was quite good at managing currency risk, the company eventually realized that Microsoft was better positioned to manage the risks associated with doing business in so many foreign currencies. The companies turned to relationship-first thinking. They quickly determined that it was best for Microsoft to manage currency fluctuations; that particular scope was turned back to Microsoft.

Another common problem happens when companies allocate work. Buying companies will frequently want to maintain "control" and often keep a shadow organization on staff to manage (or worse, micromanage) the service provider. Likewise, service providers typically want to get as much work as possible. A better approach is to determine whether the company or the service provider is best suited for the work.

Loyalty obliges the parties to choose solutions that incur the least costs for the relationship. That may mean allowing the service provider to make more profit, while it continues to streamline processes to reduce the number of people doing the work, for example.

When talking about this aspect of loyalty, we often get quizzical looks. Executives with buying companies ask, "How in the world can I justify allowing a service provider to make more profit?" While on the supplier side, executives ask, "What do you mean work to reduce the number of people servicing this account?" If parties are not thinking about the relationship, then they cannot achieve more profit and fewer people doing the work. If, however, companies apply a WIIFWe mindset, they will find ways to become more efficient so long as they don't lose money in the process.

### The Relationship Has Its Own Interests

In typical negotiations parties attempt to reconcile their interests, but if only individual interests are reconciled, the parties have not really gotten to We. The relationship can only begin to thrive when the parties realize that the relationship has its own set of interests separate from the parties' self-interests.

To illustrate, one chief procurement officer often stated emphatically, "I don't know if I have a good deal unless I go to market!"[25] At the same time the service provider's chief financial officer proclaimed it had been balancing losses on some lines of business with other, more profitable line of business. Despite a six-year relationship with phenomenal customer satisfaction scores, the companies' relationship was based on trying to reconcile their self-interests. Unfortunately that led the buying company to think it could get a better deal from another service provider, while the service provider used profits from one line of business to support the other, less profitable business offerings.

Only by being loyal to the relationship as its own entity did the companies begin to realize the limiting nature of a focus on reconciling self-interests. Once they shifted the focus to the relationship, treating each other's interests with equal concern, they realized the power they could unleash to cut costs (without the service provider taking a loss) and look for opportunities to innovate. Not only would the buying company not use resources to bid work when the service provider was meeting and exceeding expectations, it could use its resources to finally address the inefficiencies in its own operations by streamlining work with the service provider. At one point an executive from the buying company said, "I could save $1 million in unnecessary redundancies from that one suggestion [from the service provider]."[26]

Examples of disloyal behaviors abound. Frequently, one party expects the other to be loyal to the relationship, but is unwilling to reciprocate. The downward spiral of WIIFMe thinking usually starts like this: the buying company demands loyalty from the service provider throughout the duration of the contract. But as the contract draws to an end, the company puts the work out to bid, thus demonstrating zero loyalty to the service provider, which in many cases has performed as promised. The buyer justifies its actions saying, "We need to be competitive in the market."

Another example is in longer-term contracts, where the buying company might use contract renewal as a weapon at the midpoint of the contract cycle to demand further price concessions. And another example occurs when service providers assign their most qualified team members to the buyer, but shortly after transitioning the work, replace them with less qualified workers. The service provider justifies its actions by saying, "We are not making any money on this deal and have to put our best people on other more profitable accounts." These examples perpetuate the lack of loyalty to the relationship.

*Elimination of Information Asymmetries*

Chapter 3 discusses how transparency and openly sharing information can build trust. Unfortunately, most business relationships are plagued with information asymmetries where data is typically unequally distributed between the parties. According to the Nobel laureate Douglass North, this lack of information leads to higher transaction costs since information is needed to understand how to value goods and services.[27]

Most often, the cheapest and thus the best way for the parties to eliminate any information asymmetries is to simply share information. Information-sharing—transparency and openness—is required by the principle of loyalty. Loyalty obliges the parties to show a great deal of transparency since that will decrease the overall transaction costs for the relationship. The benefit of increased transparency and openness is trust and a better decision-making process.

## Expressing Intentions about Loyalty

Very few companies talk about loyalty to their relationships. Traditional transaction-based relationships do not oblige loyalty. Therefore, defining loyalty regarding the relationship will break new ground. Parties who have taken the time to acknowledge loyalty to the relationship have seen greater unity and dedication to a shared vision.

Here are some topics for discussion to help companies understand and define loyalty to the relationship:

---

**Topics to Define and Understand Loyalty to the Relationship**

- What are your (each person's) impressions of how your team/ company could show loyalty to the relationship?
- What are your (each person's) impressions of how your partner's team/company could show loyalty to the relationship?
- What barriers to relationship loyalty (frequent bidding and RFP's/ frequent personnel reorganization) does this relationship face and from which party?

- Who should be included in conversations about the meaning of relationship loyalty (i.e., procurement or sourcing professionals, sales, legal, etc.)?
- What steps should we take to better understand and allocate risks to the party best able to manage and mitigate risk?
- Have we allocated work to the wrong party and how should we handle reallocation of workloads?
- How can we (the relationship) eliminate information asymmetries and make the relationship more transparent and open?

The answers will help the companies understand how they will embody loyalty to the relationship. As people from each company participate in this conversation, look for common themes, words, or feelings. These common themes and words would then go into a statement of intention regarding loyalty to the relationship. For example, a statement of intent regarding loyalty might read like this:

### Suggested Statement of Intent: Loyalty to the Relationship

*In keeping with the obligation of loyalty to the relationship, we will strive to value the other party's interests to the same extent that we value our own individual interests. We will always treat the parties' interests with equal concern. We will seek ways to make the relationship fair and balanced by [include specific measures here regarding risk mitigation and allocation, workload allocation, and the free flow of information]. By working together while acknowledging the relationship, each party stands the best chance of reaching its vision for the future.*

Relationship-first thinking is the cornerstone theme of this statement of intent. Since this is a new way of looking at loyalty, each company should really understand this concept and get buy-in from all relevant stakeholders. The idea is to document this intention because some people may find it difficult to show the relationship loyalty by their actions.

## EQUITY

Business people tend to view a relationship in balance sheet terms. Each side should be equal. This is especially true in Western societies where equality is a fundamental social norm. The principle of equity, however, obliges parties to look more critically at the distribution of resources. It might be easy to split things fifty-fifty, but it might not be fair.

Equity is also a legal principle arising out of the limitations of English common law many centuries ago. Most people don't use the word equity, but they do understand the concept. Often, people talk of fairness when they really mean equity. While it is unusual for a business person to use the word equity, high-performing relationships adhere to the principle nonetheless.

## Two Aspects of Equity

Equity has two equally important components: *proportionality* and *remedies*. Proportionality means one party may get a larger distribution of rewards (remedy) than the other to compensate that party for taking greater risks or making investments (proportionality). An equitable remedy allows the parties to come to a fair resolution when the contract itself may otherwise limit the result or be silent on the matter. For example, the contract might inadequately address the service provider's performance requirements during a catastrophic natural disaster, such as a Category 4 hurricane. Any resulting ambiguity should be discussed with the principle of equity in mind.

Equity is important to maintain harmony and trust in a relationship. Equitable decisions prove that a party is trustworthy and trusting at the same time precisely because the decision is not an arbitrary fifty-fifty split.

### *Proportionality*
The principle of equity obliges parties to share the rewards in proportion to their contributions, resources invested, and risks taken. Equity prevents tensions from arising in the relationship because the relationship can address inequalities that arise over time. Let's return to the orange story discussed in chapter 1 by way of example.

In the story of the orange, two people each want a specific part of the orange for different reasons. One person wants the peel to flavor a cake. The other person wants to eat the pulp. If each person were committed to dividing the orange equally, each would get exactly one half of the orange. As each person looks at the different parts of the orange, each might decisde that she needs only a small portion of the orange relative to the other person's share. The person who wants to eat the pulp might get all of the pulp, while the person who wants the peel might only get as much as needed for the cake recipe.

To take the story to the next step, how should these two people share the orange if the person who wants the peel bought the orange? These are the types of questions that business people face when applying the principle of equity. Companies have developed ways of addressing proportionality in many ways, and the Creative Value Allocation process is discussed in chapter 8.

Clients usually refer to proportionality as "fairness." Splitting things fifty-fifty is easy, and at least one scholar's research finds that companies default to equal splits to maintain harmony in a relationship.[28] Splitting cost savings fifty-fifty would certainly bolster the principle of loyalty to the relationship. However, a fifty-fifty split is not always the equitable thing to do.

For example, some companies attempt various gain-sharing schemes. Gain-sharing happens when a service provider achieves predetermined cost-reduction efforts resulting in measurable savings to the customer. When the service provider reaches the targeted cost savings, ideally the customer pays the service provider a proportion of the savings. A fifty-fifty gain-share, while equal, is not necessarily equitable.

For example, an equal split of $200,000 (the total cost savings the service provider achieved for the customer) represents a different value to each party and perhaps a different level of investment also. For the buying company, a savings of $100,000 ($200,000 minus the $100,000 gain-share payment to the service provider) has a different overall meaning in a $5 million dollar total budget than for the service provider who will record its $100,000 share as pure profit since the company paid the service provider's costs (labor, overhead, etc.) in the normal course of business. Therefore, many business people tend not to split cost-reduction savings fifty-fifty but rather in some fair proportion based on risk reward allocation.

Microsoft's OneFinance team grappled with the issue of how to "share" value from transformational efforts.[29] Microsoft was buying transformation, plain and simple. In order to achieve transformation, Accenture would have to invest in processes and people to uncover and implement projects to save time and money. The OneFinance team wanted to be fair and in the end devised an equitable solution to the problem of how to distribute rewards when Accenture was contributing more up-front resources.

At first, Accenture was skittish about suggestions that it enter into a gain-sharing arrangement with Microsoft. Srini Krishna, director of global supplier management, finance operations of Microsoft Corporation, sympathized with Accenture. Frequently people fight to define their "fair share." Krishna understood that service providers become gun-shy about implementing transformation projects without properly defining the mechanism for allocating the rewards of transformative projects. Defining and documenting the value-sharing approach helped Accenture feel comfortable investing in a relationship with Microsoft.

Krishna said, "We were adamant that we wanted to formally define and develop contractual mechanisms that would make Accenture feel comfortable that if they made smart investments that created value, they would get their fair share."[30]

The companies jointly developed a simple mathematical model to compute each company's fair share of each transformation initiative. Using the model, each company can estimate its anticipated return on investment (ROI) for each initiative. Once the model was in place, it became easier to allocate the ROI. For example, Accenture's share of the ROI includes the following:

**Accenture's Share of the ROI**

- Implementation costs: those costs associated with the actual implementation of the initiative.
- Compensation for profit margin on the lost revenue (represented increased efficiencies) due to project implementation.
- Transformation incentive percentage, which is defined as a percentage of the cost savings agreed to up front.

Microsoft gets what is left after subtracting these line items from the total savings.

Andrew Cheung, the Accenture partner responsible for the OneFinance account said, "We've had the model in place since we started in February 2007, and it has never failed us. We know our fair share. It is simple. It just works. I have no hesitation to make heavy investments in Microsoft because we've proven the pricing model works—again and again."[31]

This math model helped the OneFinance team find an equitable solution to an age-old problem: how to proportionally share the rewards of transformation initiatives. Sometimes Accenture might get the larger check, sometimes Microsoft might get it. At the end of the day everyone agreed that the model produces "fair" or equitable results.

### Remedies

The other aspect of equity stems from the limitations of English common law. Hundreds of years ago, courts of chancery remedied the limitations and inflexibility of common law by supplementing common law with decisions meant to make the parties whole again. This concept shares the same name, but not the same intention as a remedy in the sense of a corrective action or sanction.

Equity in the form of a remedy that addresses contractual limitations serves a very important purpose in relationships: it allows people to do the right thing even if the contract doesn't call for that action. Two companies can try to conceive of all possible contingencies, but business happens. If the contract doesn't provide a solution, the companies may decide to find an equitable solution instead.

When P&G and JLL first struck their deal, no one contemplated that P&G would acquire Gillette, yet it did. JLL rose to the occasion by helping P&G integrate Gillette's properties into the P&G portfolio. For example, JLL performed more than 1,100 projects and 11,000 office moves. The same year JLL accomplished the Gillette transition, their year-end performance scores were lower than expected.

P&G made a decision to look at the entire situation and evaluate JLL's scores in light of the totality of the circumstances. P&G was appreciative of the Gillette success—an organization of nearly 30,000 had been integrated into the P&G platform. P&G estimated that overall synergies from the integration of the companies amounted to around

$4 million a day and the faster JLL could help with facilities integration, consolidation and moves, the quicker P&G would benefit from the acquisition. Lydia Jacobs-Horton, P&G GBS Director, global facilities and real estate, relates, "JLL did such an excellent job on Gillette properties, we were happy we had the (contractual) option to offer them a larger bonus than the scoring represented." Basically, it comes down to trust in playing fairly.[32]

P&G was acting in an equitable manner toward JLL because it took steps to remedy a situation that would have been unfair had P&G not taken into account how much the Gillette acquisition increased JLL's responsibilities in a very short time frame. In other words, JLL had earned certain scores, but P&G recognized that those scores did not tell the whole story. Having an equitable mindset, P&G awarded JLL a larger than anticipated bonus.

## Expressing Intent about Equity

Every partner wants to be fair when splitting rewards, compensating for risks taken and investments made. What parties tend to overlook is that each party has its own definition of fair, and different people within each organization will have their own version of fair.

By defining equity, each party takes responsibility for keeping the relationship in balance. Sometimes companies may get an unequal proportion of cost savings or will agree to take on different levels of risk. The key is to have a common definition to help people navigate those situations with an eye toward overall balance within the relationship.

Here are some topics for discussion to help each party understand and define equity:

> **Topics to Define Equity**
>
> - In an existing relationship, how have we tried to be "fair" when splitting the rewards of cost savings, risks taken, and investments made? When/how were those efforts successful?
> - In a new relationship, how has each party successfully tried to be "fair" when splitting the rewards of cost savings, risks taken,

and investments made with a different party? What made those efforts successful?

- What issues will trigger a conversation about proportionality rather than equality (i.e., one-sided investments made for the benefit of the relationship)?
- What governance process do we need to have in place to agree on a proportional distribution of benefits and who will have ultimate authority from each party to agree to the scheme?
- In an existing relationship, how have we (each party) addressed situations that were not defined in the contract? Would we agree to do it that way again?
- For new relationships, how has each party addressed situations that were not defined in a contract? Would that party like to replicate that process again?
- What governance process should we have to address issues that require a remedy not spelled out in the contract?

Answering these questions will help companies understand how they will approach equity. As people from each company participate in this conversation, look for common themes, words, or feelings. Just as in all the other principles, these common themes and words would then go into a statement of intention regarding equity. For example, a statement of intent regarding equity might read like this:

### Suggested Statement of Intent: Equity

*We acknowledge that some situations will require an unequal distribution of benefits for risks taken or investments made. In those situations, and in keeping with the obligation of equity, we will strive to compensate each party in proportion to the value, risk, or investment made to the relationship.*

*We further acknowledge that we will face unpredictable situations we may not have addressed in our initial contract. In keeping with this principle, we will work within our governance structure to remedy any situation not covered in the contract in a way that preserves the purpose and meaning of the parties' intentions for the relationship.*

The theme of equity is having the foresight to get the balance right and being open to creating remedies when circumstances change. At the end of the day, equity keeps the relationship in balance by not allowing one party to win at the other's expense. It also fosters flexibility and agility. Because situations requiring an equitable solution may not arise for some time, it is important to document this intention.

## INTEGRITY

Integrity adds the final ingredient to a robust relationship. The principle of integrity refers to past events when the parties were involved in similar situations. Simply stated, integrity means *consistency in decision-making and in actions.*

Intuitively, people understand this principle. People want to be able to rely on each other to make the same decision and to take the same action in the same set of circumstances. People want to know that they will get the same result from the same set of actions.

Integrity is essential to get to the We mentality and to stay there. Integrity preserves the relationship because integrity promotes trust between the parties. Integrity means that parties are trusting and trustworthy at the same time. To act with integrity is to show trustworthiness, which strengthens the foundation of the relationship. Integrity promotes predictability, since what has happened in the past says something about what can be expected to happen in the future. Integrity thus reduces complexity.

There are two obvious ways to know when integrity is missing. First, a company will face the same set of circumstances but make different decisions. Inconsistent decisions breed distrust. Second, a company's words don't match its actions.

A person of integrity will act in accordance with a consistent set of principles or convictions. Similarly, a relationship acting with integrity will abide by the guiding principles for the relationship. Just as people with integrity don't waiver, neither do We relationships when it comes to living the principles.

Consistency in decision making and in action means respecting the past. Past events tell the parties how to deal with situations in the present. Not to respect the principle of integrity is to deny the history of the business relationship, which is the same as to deny the relationship. On the other hand, respecting the principle of integrity recognizes that history and thus the relationship. This principle, therefore, preserves the relationship by fostering trust and respect.

Integrity is important to everyone, but it is a reputational entry card for high-performing relationships. If integrity is not demonstrated, it's difficult to get in the door. Over time, trust and loyalty depend on visible care for the results of what is actually done. Operating based on the letter of the contract or the letter of the law will not win hearts and minds. In other words, the contract could be overly punitive or restrictive. One executive said, "Being right and maintaining your integrity is not always enough...you need to demonstrate concern for the well-being of them [the affected parties] too."[33]

Integrity is rarely discussed as a principle governing business relationships. References to concepts such as the spirit of the contract implicitly refer to the principle of integrity.

A collaborative relationship is held together by its vision and goals as well as by core principles such as reciprocity and loyalty. The vision and goals are future-focused and give the relationship a direction forward. Principles such as autonomy, reciprocity, and equity tell the parties, among other things, how they should act in any present situation. But this is not enough to keep the relationship together. Just as a family, a friendship, or an entire nation is held together by common memories of the past, so is the business relationship.

## When Integrity Is Absent

Integrity is always important in a business relationship. When an organization changes a key individual working in the relationship, integrity becomes critical. The spirit of the relationship exists through the actions of individuals. When those individuals leave and others enter, the principle of integrity can ensure the continuity of the relationship.

For example, a relationship unfortunately was destroyed because of lack of integrity. A large company had outsourced a considerable part of its information technology (IT) functions to a service provider. The relationship was successful, and the IT service provider was named the company's Supplier of the Year. The company frequently praised the IT service provider for its loyalty to the customer and innovative attitude. For years, senior management on both sides supported the relationship.

But then there was a change in leadership at the outsourcing company. It hired a new chief information officer (CIO). While the outsourcing company had a long and successful history with the IT service provider, the new CIO did not. Furthermore, the new CIO had no intention of honoring his company's history with the IT service provider or the fact that the IT service provider was one of his company's most successful suppliers.

The new CIO quickly changed many of the rules and practices that had been developed between the parties over time. The former loyalty to the relationship was exchanged for loyalty to one of the parties—the buying company. This of course provoked reactions from the IT service provider, whose loyalty also turned from the relationship to itself. Trust quickly faded.

Eventually, the company terminated the contract. A successful business relationship went into a virtual death spiral because the new CIO did not apply integrity to the relationship.[34]

## Expressing Intent about Integrity

Every company thinks it acts with integrity. Naturally, people will look for ways to justify why they are not making the same decision when presented with the same set of facts or why their behavior is not aligned with their expressed wishes. The purpose of discussing and defining integrity it to keep everyone committed to living according to the best interest of the relationship.

Here are some topics for discussion to help each company understand and define integrity:

**Topics to Define Integrity**

- In an existing relationship, how have we perceived our partner as not acting with integrity either by saying one thing and doing another or by making arbitrary decisions?

- In a new relationship, how have we perceived our partner as not acting with integrity either by saying one thing and doing another or by making arbitrary decisions?
- What impact did the lack of integrity have on the relationship and the business at hand (day-to-day operations)?
- Are there certain types of issues that tend to trigger behaviors that do not show integrity? What should we do to prevent those issues from happening?
- How do we want to hold people accountable when we perceive that person is not acting with integrity?

The answers likely will reveal underlying (and usually unspoken) flaws in the relationship. For example, people might be aligned but the contract is not aligned with intentions. Or people at the highest level are aligned, but the people who report to them are not.

As people from each company participate in this conversation, look for common themes, words, or feelings. This discussion can open a can of worms. It is important to have the conversation, however, because not having it means delay and doesn't solve the issues. Just as in all the other principles, any common themes and words would then go into a statement of intention regarding integrity. For example, a statement of intent regarding integrity might go like this:

**Suggested Statement of Intent: Integrity**

*Integrity is a fundamental principle that enables companies to trust in each other's words and actions. We will continually strive to make decisions that are consistent with decisions made in the past in similar situations. Furthermore, we acknowledge that in order for the relationship to achieve extraordinary results, individuals must align their words and their actions. We will not tolerate arbitrary decision-making, nor will we allow one person (or several people) to say one thing while doing another. Our collective words and actions will be aligned for the greater good of the relationship.*

The theme is consistency. Integrity builds trust and decreases uncertainty.

## Documenting the Principles

Now that there is agreement on the meaning and purpose of the principles, it's time to document them in the form of a statement of intent. Because the six guiding principles are integral to the WIIFWe philosophy, they ought to be formalized in writing in either a memorandum of understanding or an attachment to the contract. Physically documenting the principles—and appending them to the contract itself—shows that the discussions about the principles are not hollow promises made when times were good. It also helps ensure that intentions are not lost when key people transition away from working on the relationship.

Many companies ask if they should apply (or document) the principles to existing relationships. The answer is yes, because one cannot assume that the principles will automatically be adopted as new players enter the relationship. One company that has taken the time to document and describe the desired behavior for their business relationships is McDonald's. Gary Johnson, senior director of McDonald's worldwide supply chain, leads a joint McDonald's/supplier team to document and describe desired behaviors—known as the Value of Supply Chain. Johnson explains the importance of doing this even though core principles had been embedded into their culture for decades. "While we had a legacy of how we behaved, we did not have a formal written document that codified our approach. We wanted both McDonald's and our suppliers to understand how behaviors provide a competitive advantage to the (McDonald's) System. And behaviors start with us. Just by having suppliers take a seat at the table, McDonald's demonstrates the importance and that McDonald's/supplier interactions are a critical part of the discussion."

### *Process for Documenting the Principles*
This chapter has provided guidance regarding the principles organizations should negotiate as foundational elements of their relationship. What is not prescribed in detail is how to go about getting a consensus on them. A process similar to the process for creating a shared vision statement is recommended. While one party can take the lead, the process must be completed collaboratively. One way to do this is to have cross-functional teams comprised of a mix of senior and middle management and ranging from operations to legal. Small groups

of two to five people (with representatives from each company) should go through and answer the topics for discussion associated with each principle and then craft a statement of intention for that principle. The sample language provides good guidance for crafting the statement of intent for each principle.

Companies should consider having a professional facilitator help walk them through each principle. Using a Certified Deal Architect is one option to assist companies as they agree upon and document the guiding principles. Certified Deal Architects are neutral third parties. Professional facilitators who are also impartial give the parties involved the opportunity to stay focused and put day-to-day business aside.

Combine the draft of the principles with the draft shared vision. A small team from each company should establish a project plan to roll out and institutionalize the newly established cultural norms for the relationship.

Are you ready to get started? If so, the box outlines a checklist to consider as you set out to establish the principles that will become the foundation of the relationship.

### Checklist for Negotiating the Principles

- What stakeholders and what functions need to help develop the principles?
- Should the meeting be held on-site or off-site?
- Who will facilitate the process? An internal or external resource?
- Will an internal facilitator also need to participate in the vision process as a stakeholder?
- Realistically, how much time can each party dedicate to the process?
- What preparatory work should each party complete before attending the meeting?
- Who will take the principles and gather buy-in from other team members?
- How will principles be institutionalized into the culture of how the parties behave on a daily basis?

## The Next Leg

You've successfully negotiated the foundational principles that will guide the relationship. It's now time to jointly develop a flexible framework for achieving the vision while applying the guiding principles.

# STEP 4: NEGOTIATING AS WE

The first three steps in the Getting to We process are complete. Companies are building a relationship based on strong foundation of trust, transparency, and compatibility. They have also jointly created a shared vision and negotiated the six guiding principles that will drive collaborative behaviors. Now, the next step: they are ready to negotiate the deal specifics, such as the exchange of goods and/or services. This section provides the tools and techniques for negotiating as We.

Parties following the Getting to We process *must not start* by negotiating the details of the deal such as the scope of work, pricing, and terms and conditions. Rather, they must first establish the mechanisms they will jointly use as they negotiate those details. Negotiating as We emphasizes transparency and adherence to a process that allows parties to stand on equal footing. Therefore, step 4 includes three elements that distinguish negotiating as We from all other conventional, transaction-based negotiations. Each element is discussed in the following three chapters.

Chapter 6 provides suggestions for establishing and following certain rules for negotiating highly collaborative relationships. The companies must agree to abide by these rules in advance. This ensures that the way each party negotiates supports continuous collaboration while discussing the details of the deal.

Chapter 7 compares conventional WIIFMe negotiating strategies and tactics with WIIFWe strategies and tactics. It provides tips to help negotiators understand that negotiation style, strategies, and tactics can either support or undermine collaborative efforts.

Chapter 8 offers a framework for helping parties exchange value in a fair and balanced manner in order to provide long-term mutual benefits for them. This chapter is especially helpful for parties negotiating monetary issues and allocating risks and rewards.

The Getting to We approach to negotiating is much more expansive than negotiations typified by conversations about prices, scope of work, or contractual terms and conditions. Furthermore, in long-term relationships, negotiations also occur when unforeseen circumstances happen, such as natural disasters, economic downturns, and market fluctuations. Each of these circumstances will require the parties to renegotiate some—or perhaps many—aspects of the deal to keep the relationship focused on achieving the vision in a mutually beneficial manner.

Many people view the tough discussions resulting from changed circumstances—or even the seemingly simple discussions that business people have on a daily basis—as not being negotiations. But they are negotiations. Decisions such as addressing a natural disaster, changing metrics, or staffing for increased growth are all negotiations. Any discussion and resulting decision that may impact the relationship or economic balance in the relationship is a negotiation.

For this reason, think of negotiating as We as an ongoing process that occurs throughout the life of the relationship. With this in mind, it is now time to craft the mechanisms used to negotiate the specifics of the deal.

# CHAPTER 6

# FOUR RULES FOR COLLABORATIVE NEGOTIATIONS

M any negotiation experts refer to negotiations as a game. Chester L. Karrass is one of those experts. His book *The Negotiating Game*,[1] published in 1992, sets the stage for very traditional transaction-based negotiations. Karrass and other experts have taught the same rules of engagement for negotiating deals for decades. But what people fail to understand is that business has changed dramatically in the past twenty years, and the rules for negotiating deals also need to change.

Negotiating interdependent, value-driven relationships requires business people to set aside the old ways of doing things and embrace a new way. Collaborative negotiations have their own set of rules. More important, the parties must agree to follow the rules.

There are four inviolable rules. First, the parties must sit side by side and face the issues together. Second, the parties should always follow the six guiding principles—there are no exceptions. Third, the parties should develop a flexible framework to achieve the shared vision that allows parties to remain stable and adaptable to changing circumstances. Fourth, when there is a conflict between achieving a goal and following one of the six principles, choose to follow the principle and find another way to meet the goal. Each rule is discussed below.

These rules must be clearly communicated and agreed upon by all stakeholders. And every stakeholder must understand that not following the rules is the equivalent of cheating.

Negotiators will likely find that they may need to include rules specific to the relationship. The goal is to identify and document any additional negotiating rules the parties intend to follow. And if the rules are not working, then stop to understand why. Never simply disregard the rules, as this could also be considered cheating.

Robert Axelrod's tit-for-tat findings, as discussed in chapter 1, are particularly helpful when considering any rules in addition to these four rules negotiators will use to reach a highly collaborative agreement.[2] Parties will mirror what the other does, and this is especially true when negotiating the details of any deal. Moreover, continuous cooperation needs successive cooperative moves by the parties. One "defection" can trigger the competitive tit-for-tat escalation of ever-increasing competitive behavior. Therefore, collaborative negotiation rules inspire parties to make continuous cooperative moves.

## RULE 1: SIT SIDE BY SIDE, FACE THE ISSUES TOGETHER

Companies that embrace a WIIFWe mindset don't face each other across the negotiating table in a traditional tug-of-war. Instead, they metaphorically sit side-by-side, facing the issues together. Now that the parties have agreed to work together to achieve a shared vision, it naturally follows that they will negotiate the details of making that vision a reality together.

The concept of sitting on the same side of the table is not new. *Getting to Yes*,[3] for example, recommends that the parties sit side by side when negotiating. This is known as joint problem solving. But while it is true that the negotiators are trying to solve problems, they are still coming at the problems from a WIIFMe mindset. Negotiators use *Getting to Yes*'s problem solving tactics to better achieve their own goals, not as a method for achieveing the relationship's goals.

Sitting side-by-side means that parties acknowledge that the relationship also has its own interests. This is the crux of the WIIFWe philosophy. And that philosophy permeates all the negotiation conversations that people will have throughout the term of the relationship.

One highly collaborative relationship realized the true power in sitting side-by-side when facing issues.[4] The service provider was not going to make an important IT deadline despite its best efforts to do so. Missing the deadline was going to cause some significant problems for its client—a telecom company. The service provider's account director, Jack, was preparing to face his client's vice president alone to report the bad news. Jack was fully expecting a heated exchange about the reasons for the missed deadline. Instead, something else happened.

The day before the meeting between Jack and the vice president, Jack got a call from Sam, the client's IT director. Sam suggested that he and Jack meet to discuss the meeting with the vice president. He told Jack, "We're in this together and we need to figure it out together. I'm not going to throw you under the bus now." Jack and Sam met to renegotiate several aspects of the project, including a revised work flow and project schedule. Then they went to the meeting with the vice president together.

After Jack and Sam discussed the missed deadline and the revised plan to finish the project in a timely manner, Jack said, "He [the vice president] just shrugged his shoulders and said 'ok.' I was surprised and I knew at the moment that we were working together as one team." It was a turning point in the relationship because all the stakeholders embodied the WIIFWe mindset. Sitting side-by-side to face the problem together meant that each party was negotiating from the point of view of the best interest of the relationship between Jack's company and Sam's company.

## Topics for Discussion

- What philosophical changes will have to take place to metaphorically sit side-by-side with the other party to negotiate?
- Will we have to brief more people on the collaborative nature of the negotiations? If so, who?
- What corporate policies (whether written or unwritten) may impact sitting side-by-side rather than across the table from one another?

## RULE 2: LET THE PRINCIPLES GUIDE BEHAVIOR

Companies should *apply all of the guiding principles to all negotiations*. The six essential principles guide the parties' behaviors as they negotiate everything, from the contract to annual reporting metrics or project plans. It is critical to remember that the principles drive collaborative behaviors. This is equally true for existing relationships and for new relationships. Therefore, to ensure a constant state of collaboration each party is responsible for following the principles all the time.

For example, if the parties take seriously the principle of loyalty, they will look out for the interests of the relationship, which means that some very common ways in which companies currently negotiate become questionable.

Coercion is one tactic that violates the principles. Coercion is any threat of penalty that induces one partner to agree in order to avoid the consequences. By responding to the threat, however, the partner is acting against its self-interest.[5] For example, one way that parties might choose to coerce each other is in threatening to leave the relationship: a powerful buyer might coerce a supplier to lower its prices by threatening to switch the work to the supplier's competitor. This type of coercion is not in the best interest of a collaborative relationship seeking to achieve a shared vision, and it puts the economics of the deal out of balance.

By following the principle of reciprocity, the parties will make a fair and balanced exchange to ensure that all parts of the relationship are in accordance with the principle of equity. This is how they solve the frequent tension between creating and claiming value in the relationship, as discussed in chapter 8.

As an example, the OneFinance deal between Microsoft and Accenture[6] structured the most potentially divisive negotiations—incentive payments—for continuous collaboration. Microsoft wanted innovative ideas and processes from Accenture; therefore, Microsoft and Accenture agreed on a pricing model that incorporated incentive payments for projects that transformed processes to be more cost-effective and efficient for Microsoft. The companies adopted a mathematical formula that was simple yet balanced. Microsoft and Accenture leveraged all the guiding principles in the process of negotiating the incentive model.

**OneFinance Followed the Principles**

**Reciprocity**—Under the incentive model, Microsoft and Accenture are both winners. The pre-established calculations for the model determine a fair way to share benefits between Microsoft and Accenture. Reciprocity is built into the system.

**Autonomy**—Accenture has the latitude to find creative, innovative solutions to deliver on the much desired transformation Microsoft sought.

**Honesty**—The companies input accurate information to the incentive payment math formula; neither company tries to game the system with inaccurate information.

**Loyalty**—Accenture and Microsoft have a governance structure that keeps the parties aligned to the interests of the relationship in choosing the transformation projects to pursue.

**Equity**—They agreed early in the partnering process that Accenture would be compensated for a period of time for lost profit margin on work that it no longer performed as a result of its own transformation projects.

**Integrity**—The incentive payment model is an agreed mathematical formula, thus the results are predictable for Microsoft and Accenture.

Because Microsoft and Accenture applied all of the principles during their negotiations to devise the incentive payment formula, what could be hotly debated money conversations became cooperative conversations. This is different from conventional negotiations that many business people are familiar with. Microsoft and Accenture also used a different set of techniques to reach their agreement.

**Topics for Discussion**

- How will we live by each guiding principle during negotiations?
- How will we hold people accountable if they don't apply one of the principles during negotiations?

- How will we verify that the total agreement embodies all the guiding principles?

## RULE 3: DEVELOP A FLEXIBLE FRAMEWORK
## TO ACHIEVE THE SHARED VISION

All highly collaborative relationships face a common challenge: how to achieve the shared vision. Creating a flexible yet stable framework for the relationship is the key to success. Rather than documenting every contingency in a 500-page contract, the parties look to develop an agreement that provides sufficient detail without becoming overly prescriptive.[7]

The parties will negotiate the exchange of goods and services. As was mentioned, this is the point where most conventional negotiations begin. It is not the beginning of highly collaborative relationships, however. The parties will still have to find out what work is needed, how to allocate the work, how to deal with identified risks, and how to find a pricing model that gives the parties the right incentives to work toward the vision and goals to the benefit of the relationship. These decisions will be distilled into a flexible framework—an actual contract—or a less formal memorandum of understanding between two divisions within one company.

*What* the framework includes depends on the specific relationship. Although details will always depend on the nature of the relationship, parties will maintain their focus on achieving the shared vision and goals and objectives.

Some executives balk at the thought of making a long-term commitment. Most companies have little idea what their future will look like in three, five, or ten years. One executive said, "We don't know where our business will be in two years, so we don't want to commit ourselves to a five-year agreement with our service provider."[8] Rarely will any business executives know with certainty where their business will be in a couple of years. Rather than developing a rigid one-year contract, high-performing relationships develop a flexible framework.

By developing flexible and adaptable agreement structures, buying companies feel more comfortable thinking about entering longer term agreements. Likewise, with flexibility and long-term agreements, service providers feel more comfortable making investments in the relationship.

Sometimes parties decide to cooperate on joint projects but do not know in any detail what those projects will be. For instance, some research and development (R&D) relationships face this situation. In R&D relationships several parties (including universities, governmental agencies, and private enterprises) may agree to cooperate on R&D projects in specified areas such as electricity, environmental sustainability, mobile telephony. It is not uncommon that some of the participants are competitors in some parts of the value chain. In such cases, the parties can only agree on a framework that describes how they will proceed when planning and executing specific research projects.

**Topics for Discussion**

- What does a flexible framework mean for our relationship?
- How will we ensure that all stakeholders are aware of the changes to the agreement?
- What is the right balance between flexibility and specificity for our relationship?

## RULE 4: FOLLOW THE PRINCIPLES, ADAPT THE GOALS

Situations may arise that cause a conflict between reaching a specific goal and following the guiding principles. One partner could decide that it's quicker to achieve a solution that is basically unfair to one of the parties. Or the parties could agree upon a goal that when pushed downstream to other stakeholders creates a conflict between abiding by the principles and pursuing the goal.

The following is a good example of a conflict between principles and goals in a multiparty sourcing situation. A few years ago, a customer and one of its service providers decided to adopt a WIIFWe mindset. We'll call them ABC CO and Supplier A. The parties agreed on a shared vision and goals and committed to embody the guiding principles they laid out for the relationship. Under the agreement Supplier A further agreed to work with Supplier B—an existing supplier to ABC CO—to deliver a key capability that Supplier A did not have.

ABC CO and Supplier A negotiated Supplier A's involvement with Supplier B. Supplier B became a subcontractor to Supplier A. Less than a year later, ABC CO tasked Supplier A to renegotiate ABC CO's contract with Supplier B and to seek significant cost savings on ABC CO's behalf. Supplier A did not follow the guiding principles so critical in getting a fair and balanced agreement when it was negotiating with Supplier B. Supplier A told Supplier B if it did not agree to Supplier A's demands, it would lose the work. But agreeing to the terms of the deal would mean Supplier B would lose money. Supplier B saw its participation in the cost reduction plan as a no-win situation.

This was an example of a conflict between the principles and the immediate short-term goal to reduce costs. Supplier A used coercive power to extract savings from Supplier B, and Supplier B never had the opportunity to play a role in the negotiations. Supplier B had no autonomy to make decisions in its best interest, and it could not show loyalty to the relationship because it was not a true party to the relationship between ABC CO and Supplier A. Furthermore, Supplier A was not showing loyalty to the partnership.

The relationship between Supplier A and Supplier B quickly deteriorated. Neither Supplier A nor Supplier B wanted to work with the other and placed the customer, ABC CO, in the middle of the conflict. The customer chose to grab for a short-term gain at Supplier B's expense, so it is no wonder that the relationship was contentious.

It might have been in the best interest of the relationship between ABC CO, Supplier A, and Supplier B to work to find a solution together. As it stood, Supplier B exited the relationship when its contract was up as the new financial terms were unsustainable.

Instead, the three companies should have met, realigned to the guiding principles, and renegotiated an agreement with Supplier B. Very rarely is there only one way to achieve a goal, especially when cost reduction is the goal. The parties likely would have found an alternative way to achieve cost-savings goals while still acting in accordance with the guiding principles.

Parties should always let the guiding principles prevail *unless everyone agrees otherwise (without being coerced)*. ABC CO and Supplier A chose to strictly pursue the goals and thus sacrificed the principles and put the relationship's goals at risk of not being achieved. This had disastrous results, ranging from a loss of trust to Supplier B's exit from the relationship.

Another point to remember is that in multisourcing relationships, it is wise to choose one approach—either a conventional WIIFMe mindset or a WIIFWe mindset—but not both simultaneously. Had ABC CO and Supplier A extended the principles of their relationship to Supplier B, they would have sought to negotiate a more balanced approach to meeting cost-saving goals.

**Topics for Discussion**

- How do we want to work together to adapt to a changing environment?
- How will we decide (structure and process) when it is time to change the relationship's goal(s)?
- How will we hold each other and ourselves accountable for living according to our agreed upon guiding principles when we change the relationship's goals?
- Should we ever allow deviations from the guiding principles? If so, how will we address deviations from the guiding principles and still maintain the integrity of the agreement?

Yes, it makes perfect sense to have rules for negotiating. But what about those situations that are more contentious? How will the parties still follow the rules?

## Consider Using a Neutral Party

Parties should consider using a professional facilitator as a third-party neutral voice. Many companies pay professional negotiators to help them negotiate their deal. That is a good idea, especially for complex deals where the stakes are high. But rather than use a professional negotiator, we encourage companies to consider using a third-party neutral facilitator to ensure that the parties reach a fair and balanced agreement—together.

The University of Tennessee's College of Business comprehensive Certified Deal Architect (CDA) program is one of several options for teaching the skills necessary to achieve a sound relationship based on a fair and balanced agreement.[9] There are two types of CDAs. Some work for one company, often in the procurement, account management, or contracting departments. They help coach and shepherd deals through the process of reaching a Vested agreement on behalf of their company.

Other CDAs are independent neutrals who coach the parties through the process of reaching an agreement. At a minimum, parties should consider using someone who has no dog in the hunt, so to speak, whether it is a person from within or outside the company. A different perspective from someone who is well-versed in the WIIFWe mindset and Getting to We process is critical for reaching a long-term agreement that is *mutually beneficial*.

## Negotiating as We in Action

Negotiating as We is different. Not only do parties embrace the mindset, they also follow the four negotiation rules. It does not matter if companies are entering a new relationship or changing the nature of an existing relationship. What is important is that organizations adopt a WIIFWe mindset and follow the Getting to We process. The Rocky Flats closure project shows how the US Department of Energy (DOE) and Kaiser-Hill adhered to the negotiating rules outlined in this chapter.[10]

The DOE's Rocky Flats Closure Project demonstrates how the entire web of relationships embodied the WIIFWe mindset. The project—known as a shining pillar of success in the DOE—has earned accolades from the Government Accountability Office as well as winning numerous awards. Awards are nice, but results are even better. The level of cooperation between federal, state, local governments, community groups, and Kaiser-Hill was unprecedented and led to the closure of Rocky Flats 65 years ahead of schedule (10 years versus the expected 75 years) and saved $30 billion in taxpayer dollars.[11]

The Rocky Flats story was profiled in *Vested: How P&G, McDonald's, and Microsoft are Redefining Winning in Business Relationships*. DOE and Kaiser-Hill—the contractor—followed all five of the Vested rules. But their success could not have been accomplished without taking the first step, metaphorically choosing to walk through the Vested doorway by embracing a WIIFWe mindset.

As stated previously, in a truly collaborative business arrangement the relationship *is* the substance. The relationship thus should be protected as much as possible from the inevitable tensions arising when the guiding principles are not followed. Rocky Flats exemplifies the power of embracing a WIIFWe mindset. The box below provides a sampling of how the parties followed the four negotiation rules.

> **Rocky Flats Followed the Four Negotiation Rules**
>
> **Rule 1: Sit side-by-side, face the challenge together.** The relationship between the DOE and Kaiser-Hill did not start as the most high-performing partnership. Long before Kaiser-Hill was selected to lead the cleanup efforts, the DOE and many other governmental and nongovernmental agencies battled about the cleanup efforts and the site's future. A federal court ordered the state and federal governmental agencies to work together to find a solution to the problems plaguing the site.[12]
>
> Nevertheless, once the court decree was in place, all the parties, including Kaiser-Hill, embraced the process and moved from fighting each other to fighting together to achieve success in one of the world's largest nuclear cleanup efforts. The spirit of togetherness remained for the duration of the agreement.
>
> **Rule 2: Let the principles guide behavior.** The principles were documented in 2000. Specific language was included in the agreement to break long practiced paradigms. This included language such as, "Seek ways to accelerate cleanup actions and eliminate unnecessary tasks and reviews by requiring that the Parties to the Agreement work together."[13]
>
> **Rule 3: Develop a flexible framework to achieve the shared vision.** While clear benchmarks and priorities were established, contract language remained sufficiently general; flexibility was built-in and innovation was expected. Kaiser-Hill reserved "the right to change the PCS (project control system) as required to satisfy

business purposes while staying committed to providing the level of control."[14]

**Rule 4: Follow the principles, adapt the goals.** Kaiser-Hill and the DOE entered into a second contract that modified Kaiser-Hill's incentive payment structure to meet aggressive cost-saving goals. Kaiser-Hill accepted more financial risk for not meeting established cost and performance targets. Yet Kaiser-Hill and the government applied the principles when negotiating to maintain an equitable distribution of incentive payments commensurate with Kaiser-Hill's level of investment and increased risk.

## The Next Element in Negotiating as We

It is one thing to agree on the four negotiation rules in this chapter, but it is another thing to follow them in all negotiations from the most strategic to the daily interactions. Once the parties agree to follow the rules, they are ready to move on the next chapter, which focuses on choosing negotiation strategies and tactics that embrace the WIIFWe mindset.

# CHAPTER 7

# WIIFWE STYLES, STRATEGIES, AND TACTICS

Previous chapters have noted there are hundreds of books on negotiations. Most negotiation books focus on teaching styles, strategies, and tactics. But focusing on strategies and tactics first will not work when negotiating a highly collaborative relationship.

This chapter focuses on three very important aspects of negotiating under a We mindset: First, the negotiation style people choose has a huge impact on not only the negotiations, but also the relationship. Second, people make critical decisions when they choose a strategy, so negotiation strategies must be aligned with the WIIFWe mindset. Finally, tactics must support—not undermine—the collaborative atmosphere during negotiations.

There are clear distinctions between negotiating styles, strategies, and tactics that are premised upon the conventional WIIFMe mindset rather than the WIIFWe process of Getting to We. Many conventional styles, strategies, and tactics undermine trust and conflict with the six guiding principles outlined in chapter 5.

## STYLE MATTERS

Certain contracting styles can have lasting financial and emotional results. For example, companies that foster goodwill during business negotiations, only to send in the lawyers to play hardball late in the game, risk significantly increasing transaction costs and decreasing trust. A senior executive from a computer components manufacturer once bragged, "I come in late [to the negotiations] and tend to start with the unreasonable request. My job is to relieve the anxiety of the business units from being the bad cop to get the best deal for our company."[1] In other words, this person bragged about using a muscular approach so his colleagues could give the service provider the appearance of being reasonable.

Alternatively, companies that consciously choose the right style for the right set of circumstances will reach a mutually beneficial long-term agreement. Oliver Williamson, the economist and Nobel laureate, described three contracting styles—muscular, benign and credible—as explained in chapter 2. Potential partners should each consider their contracting styles before embarking on the journey to We. Just as companies with mismatched cultures will find it difficult to develop a highly collaborative relationship, companies that use the wrong contracting style will also find it difficult to get to We.

## Muscular

In the muscular approach to contracting one partner holds the power and does not hesitate to use it. While buying companies and service providers in theory can both hold power positions, more often than not it is the buying organization that uses its power to get what it wants. Unfortunately, some companies use a heavy-handed approach in dealing with their suppliers simply because they can.

According to Williamson, the muscular approach to contracting is myopic and inefficient.[2] He further notes, "muscular buyers not only use their suppliers, but they often 'use up' their suppliers and discard them."[3] Williamson's point is that bullied suppliers will devise overt and covert options to protect themselves.

## Benign

The benign approach assumes that the parties will cooperate; both parties will give and take in the relationship. Theoretically, this approach could work in highly developed, interdependent partnerships with a long history of trust and adherence to a common set of principles.

However, in practice, the benign style often leads to passivity, which can then quickly lead to complacency. Additionally, without a long track record of fairness, the benign style can be interpreted as gullibility. In many partnerships, when the stakes are raised, the temptation to take advantage of the other party becomes too great. Robert Axelrod's findings on tit-for-tat strategies, as discussed in chapter 1, show that once one party takes advantage of the other ("defects"), the other will follow suit, thus ending cooperation until one party takes the lead to cooperate again.[4]

## Credible

The credible approach is both hardheaded and wise. It is hardheaded because it strives for clear results and accountability, but it is not mean-spirited, as is often the case with the muscular type. The credible style is wise because complex contracts are "incomplete and thus pose cooperative adaptation needs" and require the exercise of feasible foresight, meaning that "they look ahead, uncover potential hazards, work out the mechanism, and factor these back into contractual design."[5] In other words, negotiators need to use a style that will foster an atmosphere of cooperation, which will help the parties structure a flexible and adaptable agreement.

The credible style will produce a result that is fair to both parties, and it will challenge organizations to focus energy on unlocking inefficiencies rather than on negotiating for the win at the other party's expense.

Some negotiators are quite adaptable, using one style in one type of deal and another style with another type of deal. The ability to work with a range of styles is good. However, partners should avoid mixing styles within the same deal. "Too often, companies reason that there can never be too many ways to make money, and they decide to play the cooperative and competitive games at the same time. But that tactic doesn't work, because the two approaches require diametrically different behavior," Marshall L. Fisher wrote in a *Harvard Business Review* article.[6]

For example, companies will send in hard-nosed negotiators who use a muscular style to get a "good deal" and then assign the task of building the relationship to an account manager, who uses the benign style. However, there is a huge price to pay for that game in the form of trust. People tend to gloss over the fact that the tone (whether competitive or collaborative) trickles down to the day-to-day people who work together. Moreover, a competitive tone is usually very hard to change later on.

## WHAT'S YOUR STYLE?

There are many books that push for the muscular approach to negotiating agreements. These books are replete with justifications, admonishments, and real-life examples to support the premise that the muscular style gets the best deal.

For highly collaborative relationships, the muscular style won't work. What if negotiation teams make headway toward building trust by sharing information, only to have a self-described shark from one company circling until the time is right to seize an opportunity to strike? For example, after months of congenial negotiations, a hard-nosed negotiator—who has not been part of the negotiations—will swoop in at the eleventh hour to demand a price concession from the service provider. All the efforts at building a We relationship are lost. Fortunately, most negotiators, and especially people attracted to the WIIFWe mindset, are not negotiation sharks. Yet, the temptation to grab the quick gain is very powerful.

Here are some issues to consider when forming a team to negotiate and develop a highly collaborative relationship. These issues pertain equally to internal and external partnerships.

**What's Your Style?**

- Do I, or my colleagues, use negotiation tactics that overtly seek to:
  - undermine trust
  - cause uncertainty or unease
  - bully (coerce) the other side into an agreement (no matter how minor) that is not in their best interest
  - intentionally shut down conversations or problem-solving sessions

- Is there a tacit understanding at our company that someone, or a department such as legal, will enter the deal at some point to exert power to "get a better deal"?
- Do I or my colleagues minimize the impact of the muscular approach on trust?

Old habits die hard, and some "deal makers" have been using a power-based negotiation style for a long time and see no need to change. However, it is unwise and potentially a waste of time and resources to say that a company is ready to develop a highly collaborative relationship while using a power-based style to negotiate the relationship. In fact, companies with those self-described sharks on their team should reign them in or replace them with people more suited to working in a collaborative environment.

## WE STRATEGIES

Negotiation strategies provide direction for the parties to come to an agreement to achieve the relationship's goals. Strategies align the techniques and methods, usually referred to as tactics, with the goals of the negotiation.

In a conventional contract negotiation each party has its own strategy. Those strategies often emphasize a WIIFMe mindset and the corresponding tactics. For example, a buyer's goal might be to lower the overall costs of facilities management by 10 percent over three years. Its negotiation strategy would be to work with the existing provider to maintain, if not increase, the scope of work while also reducing prices over a three-year term. The buyer's tactics might also include bluffing about moving the business to a competitor if the incumbent does not lower its prices, or omitting details about a new "no catering for meetings" policy that will reduce the suppliers volumes significantly and ultimately impact the service provider's management fee.

Getting to We strategies are "together" strategies and the results are what's best for the individual partners *and* for the relationship. Since the WIIFWe mindset is different from the mindset found in traditional negotiations, strategies will also be different. The three examples that follow demonstrate the difference between a WIIFMe strategy and a WIIFWe strategy. This list is not comprehensive; rather it is meant to stimulate the thinking process when choosing a strategy to negotiate with other parties.

## Contract Between Two Partners

A typical partnership negotiation is a contract formalizing a business relationship between two independent companies. Most business people, ranging from entrepreneurs to CEOs of multinational companies, have negotiated some sort of contract in the course of their career. As a result, they believe they know the most effective way to negotiate a contract. Unfortunately, traditional contract negotiation methods tend to reinforce the WIIFMe mindset. Therefore, it is worthwhile to discuss the WIIFWe and WIIFMe strategies that successful partners use to reach an agreement, as outlined in figure 7.1.

These are not the only strategies, but they are the most common. Thus, companies can have the most positive impact by applying the guiding principles to these situations.

Of course, contract negotiations are not limited to two parties. Multiple parties also can combine energies to achieve a shared vision.

Figure 7.1    We and Me strategies

| WIIFWe Strategies | WIIFMe Strategies |
|---|---|
| **Scope of Work** | |
| The parties will design services jointly to maximize the likelihood that the partnership will achieve the vision and goals. They will jointly allocate work between them by applying the principles of autonomy and loyalty, meaning, for example, that work is allocated to the party who can carry it out at the lowest cost and highest quality. | **Service Provider:** The service provider will want to have wide latitude and a lot of flexibility, and at the same time, it will want to do as little work as possible to get paid and thereby maximize its profit margin. |
| | **Buyer:** The buyer will want to get as many services as possible for the money paid. To make the service provider perform, it will pinpoint the work in detail, narrowing the service provider's discretion, while including as much as possible in the price and thereby maximize profit margin. |

Figure 7.1  Continued

| WIIFWe Strategies | WIIFMe Strategies |
|---|---|
| **Price** | |
| The parties will design a workload allocation and corresponding pricing model that gives the parties optimal incentives to work toward the vision and goals. By applying the shared guiding principles, the pricing model will be equitable and promote loyalty to the partnership and its goals. To maintain price equilibrium, the partners will allocate work to the partner most able to reduce costs. For example, if a company wants to work with its facilities management service provider to reduce energy consumption at its facilities, the company will take on the responsibility to drive energy saving initiatives with its employees, while allowing the service provider to drive energy consumption in fixtures. | **Service Provider**: The service provider will want to make as much money as possible for as little work as possible. Even if it agrees to some price-related concessions, it will seek ways to protect its profit margin in other ways. It could change the people who work on the account (substitute the C-team for the A-team that sold the account), it could cut corners, or it could claim that every little change is out of scope and warrants increased payments.<br><br>**Buyer:** The buyer will want to pay as little as possible for as much service as possible. It will use the competitive bidding process to push service providers to cut their prices, while demanding more from them. More important, the buyer will try to hide any information about how valuable the services are to it and minimize any internal issues that could increase the scope of work for the service provider. |
| **Risks** | |
| The parties allocate risks to the partner most able to mitigate the risk. For example, if one company is better at managing fluctuating currencies in a worldwide operation, then that company would manage currency exchange, regardless of whether it is the buyer or the service provider. By applying the principles of honesty, autonomy, and loyalty to the fair allocation of risk, the partners also trigger reciprocity and trust. | **Service Provider:** The service provider will avoid taking on any risk and when forced to accept risk, will include a price premium for taking on that risk. However, the service provider will not repay the buyer when the risk does not happen.<br><br>**Buyer:** The buyer will want to shift as many risks as possible to the service provider, even those risks the buyer controls. It will pay the risk premium and use that premium to justify pressure to reduce prices on the base services. |

## Relationships Among Multiple Partners

While this situation is still a contractual arrangement, and the comments outlined in figure 7.1 apply, there are other aspects of the relationship that demand a We approach. The fact that there are several parties to a business arrangement renders acting as We even more compelling.

For the sake of illustration, let's say that one customer outsourced one business function to service provider A. Service provider A could not perform the entire suite of services, so the customer contracted with service provider B for a substantial portion of the business function. The customer then introduced A to B, and told A to monitor and manage service provider B. In a WIIFMe mindset, both A and B are in a difficult position. Technically, they are competitors. But on this project, they have to act as team members at the customer's behest. Therefore, A and B will have to coordinate their efforts in a way that might make them feel vulnerable. Moreover, the customer company sees this as one project and doesn't want to hear about disputes between A and B.

Applying the We mindset, the three parties share a common vision and have shared or complementary goals. And the only way to manage the tension will be to live by a shared set of guiding principles. Ideally, this would happen at the inception of the relationship. That way, as A and B work together, they use the principles to keep self-serving behavior in check while encouraging actions that further the partnership's goals. Figure 7.2 briefly outlines the strategies involved in initiating the We relationship among several parties.

Figure 7.2    Initiating the relationship among multiple parties

| WIIFWe Strategies | WIIFMe Strategies |
|---|---|
| **Initiating the Relationship** | |
| There are two ways to get to We. The buyer and A would develop a vision, goals, and guiding principles. A would then work with B to align the partnerships' vision, goals, and guiding principles to the relationship between A and B.<br><br>   Or the buyer, A, and B would jointly develop the vision, goals, and | **Service Provider A:** A will negotiate a deal with B that maximizes its profit in the relationship. A will want to strictly outline service level agreements and then micromanage B in an effort to protect itself in the customer's eyes. A may even take a more aggressive stance with respect to service failures. |

Figure 7.2   Continued

| WIIFWe Strategies | WIIFMe Strategies |
|---|---|
| **Initiating the Relationship** | |
| guiding principles for the entire relationship.<br>   In both circumstances, all companies would allocate work according to optimize the vision and the goals for the relationship. | **Service Provider B:** B will also want to protect its profit in the relationship and could resent any cost-reduction paths that A imposes on it on the customer's behalf. Further, B will want to maintain its relationship with the customer and will find ways to circumvent the customer's relationship with A. It will guard its scope of work and either demand more money for any change or will demand that A perform all "out of scope" work. B will view any service failures as A's fault. |
| | **Customer:** Its relationship is with A and not with B, even if customer and B had a relationship. Customer will not want to manage B at all. It is paying A to manage the relationship. It wants to see one face on the project and could be perturbed by any disputes between A and B. |

## Internal Partnering for a Common Customer

Internal partnering is often considered the least contractual relationship and, ironically, the relationship most suited for a We mentality. Most professional negotiators do not consider negotiations between departments a "negotiation." Companies are increasingly faced with having to work across divisions and functions. Thus, companies enter into situations in which there are no clear lines of authority but significant accountability to the customer.

   For example, over the years a large manufacturer merged with several smaller companies that produce similar products for the aerospace industry. As a very large company, it no longer makes individual parts

Figure 7.3   Creating the team

| WIIFWe Strategies | WIIFMe Strategies |
|---|---|
| | **Creating the Team** |
| For the sake of the customer, all appropriate stakeholders would develop a vision, goals, and guiding principles for how they will work together. Use the guiding principles to create an atmosphere of ONE working for the customer, while also driving performance goals aligned with the vision for the relationship with the customer. | **Company:** Pick the person who has the strongest numbers to lead the customer's project thinking that person has the best leadership skills. Give this person much, if not all, of the accountability for the project but limited authority over anyone outside of the direct chain of command. |
| | **Project and Division Leader:** Combine a carrot with a lot of sticks to make things happen. Have a lot of meetings to demand changes from others. Have a policy that rolls initiatives down to other divisions. |
| | **Other Divisions' Leadership:** Attempt to meet the customer's needs, but allow frustration with the situation to interfere with the interpersonal relationships with the other divisions in meeting goals. After all, you weren't included in the decision-making process. |
| | **Profit and Loss Statement** |
| We have one P&L statement that is focused on the customer. No one division has the power to disrupt the flow of work to the customer in the name of making its own numbers. The team's focus on the vision and goals for the customer trigger ever increasing loyalty to the company, the customer, and its goals. The divisions will still maintain their autonomy while serving one customer. | **Company:** Has ultimate relationship with the customers. Wants an attitude and performance as one unit. Sees the project as one project, not several projects with multiple divisions. Yet, it holds each division accountable for its own numbers and performance metrics. |
| | **Lead Division A:** Division A has authority over its own P&L statement, which is different from that of Division B. It will seek to maximize its own P&L in myriad ways that could impact Division B and the customer. Any changes in production that could maximize its own P&L, even if at the expense of B, is just the price of doing business. |
| | **Division B:** Like Division A, Division B has authority over its own P&L statement, which is different from that of Division A. It will seek to maximize its own P&L in myriad ways that could impact Division A and the customer. Any changes in production that could maximize its own P&L, even if at the expense of A, is just the price of doing business. |

for its customers. Instead, plants in separate locations make parts that one plant at another location combines into a larger unit, and this larger unit is then sold to the customer.

Because the companies were separate entities and maintained their independence after the merger for many years, they had a difficult time acting as one for the sake of the customer. The divisions treated each other as the former competitors they had been.

While the traditional issues of scope of work, price, and risk are negotiated with the customer, there are a host of other issues that can interfere with a We mentality, as shown in figure 7.3.

For Getting to We strategies to be effective, negotiators have to align their tactics with a WIIFWe mindset. Many of the tactics so widely used and taught are distinctly self-serving. Therefore, negotiators should have a set of tactics to support their We strategies.

## TACTICS

Tactics are a means to an end; they are not the end in themselves. They are the incremental methods that support a negotiation strategy or approach. As mentioned above, negotiation strategies for partnerships are different from traditional negotiation strategies. While many business people are willing to change their negotiation strategy to get to We, they use the same old tactics they've always used.

### Me Tactics

Negotiators are taught to control the setting as a way to gain influence and advantage. There are dozens of tricks of the trade. For example, one common trick is for one party to take the other party to dinner and cocktails after a long day of negotiations—hoping to get the other side intoxicated so those negotiators will have a hangover the next day and then cave in on key negotiating points. Similarly, one of the authors, for example, once spent six hours without a break negotiating an agreement in a room without water. When she asked for water, she was walked to a cooler and given one four-ounce paper cup. It was a funny story until the negotiations broke down without an agreement.

The situations discussed above are known as distributive bargaining tactics, also referred to as hardball tactics. Hardball tactics are meant to put the other party at some sort of unease if not at an outright disadvantage. Interestingly, because so many people consider negotiating a game, many are willing to tolerate hardball tactics as the price they have to pay to get to a deal.

Distributitve tactics are most commonly used when negotiating about money or its equivalent. These tactics are only useful when the negotiator wants to maximize the value she gets for her company, the relationship with the other party is not important, and money is the only issue.

People seeking the We mindset should avoid using most conventional hardball tactics. The following list outlines seven common hardball negotiation tactics. The list is not comprehensive but is designed to spark an awareness of the tactics negotiators use to impact outcomes.

## Me Tactics

**Bluffing, puffery, and exaggeration of any sort.** These are hardball tactics because it so difficult for people to verify the information contained within the bluff. A typical bluff companies use is to exaggerate what other suppliers in the market are charging for their goods and services. Suppliers will typically bluff about their bottom line price by inflating it.

**Intentional ambiguity and vagueness.** This tactic makes it difficult to understand the true nature or extent of something. For example, sales people may be vague about whether a service is included in a price, while buyers may be vague about their motivations for working with the supplier.

**Pressure to close the deal.** Buyers and sellers use this tactic to put the other party at a disadvantage. People succumb to the pressure to close the deal out of fear of losing the deal or losing more time or money.

**Stonewalling.** This tactic makes it difficult for the parties to make a decision. Often people appear polite as they stall, dither, and delay. They offer seemingly plausible reasons, but in the end the party using this tactic puts pressure on the other party to agree to unfavorable terms at the last minute.

**Good cop/bad cop.** The purpose of this tactic is to catch people off-guard. After being roughed up by the bad cop, the good cop enters the scene to make peace. That peace often comes at a price.

**Lowball/Highball.** Negotiators using this tactic start ridiculously high or low, to the point of nearly insulting the other party. Ideally, this extreme offer will cause the other party to reconsider its own offer and to move closer to the lowball or highball offer.

**Profiling.** A good example is when some companies "profile" the other company's negotiators and use the profile to take advantage of a perceived weakness. Negotiators pretend to take a personal interest in their counterpart. This is different from taking a genuine interest in people in order to find common ground upon which to reach an agreement.

These tactics are often unproductive and costly in a traditional negotiation and could destroy a collaborative negotiation.

## We Tactics

Most negotiation tactics are deeply rooted in WIIFMe thinking. Therefore, parties need different tactics to get to We. Seven tactics that support a We negotiation strategy follow in the list below. This list is not all-inclusive but illustrates the difference between WIIFMe and We tactics.

**We Tactics**
- Information is power: develop shared data for accuracy and reliability
- Reveal alternatives: they are your leverage and guide creative discussions
- Leverage the six guiding principles
- Honesty is the only policy
- Leave money on the table
- Shared vision, shared agenda
- Avoid opportunism

### *Information Is Power: Develop shared*
### *Data for Accuracy and Reliability*

How often is it repeated that information is power at the bargaining table? It is the most common justification for hoarding or misusing information. Many negotiators reveal information on an as-needed basis, meaning, "I'll reveal something as I need or want something from you." Negotiators will also use information as a battering ram to get their way. Say that a service provider had a lower-than-anticipated performance score. Competitive negotiators will use that information in a coercive way to justify demands to increase service while also lowering prices.

Chapter 3 outlined the premise that unequal access to information creates a power imbalance. While it's certainly true that information is power, it's in the *sharing* of information that exponential power lies for a highly collaborative relationship. One important way that companies share information is in documenting baseline assumptions. Many high-performing relationships have found it useful to document assumptions from usage rates to tolerances for variables to the amount of executive travel required to manage the account. Documenting baseline assumptions gives the parties insight into the exact nature of the businesses. The documented assumptions provide a point of reference for modifications of work scope, pricing, or risk.

Openly sharing information follows the principles of honesty and reciprocity. It also sets the stage for integrity later in the relationship.

### *Reveal Your Alternatives, It's Your Leverage*

A Best Alternative to a Negotiated Agreement (BATNA) is the ace up the sleeve. It's a backup plan for when things don't go as anticipated during the negotiation. Everyone gets the concept, even if people don't remember the acronym. Sharing a BATNA is one important way that parties are more transparent. As mentioned in chapter 3, at least one research study concluded that negotiators who were aware of and shared their BATNA took less extreme positions, made better trade-offs and increased the size of the pie as compared to those who did not share their BATNA.[7]

In a We partnership, many partners don't have any alternatives other than to work together. And if they do have an alternative, it is not one they really want to pursue. More important, nearly all internal partnerships have little or no choice but to work together for the common good of the company. Acting as if there is an alternative, however, is misguided.

Companies that choose to reveal their alternatives, or bottom-line walkaway, are adhering to the principle of honesty, which in turn increases trust. Increased trust gives the partnership more power to address the problems the partnership is meant to address.

By working *together* in a partnership—and not playing games—the partnership creates value for each company. Together, the partnership has more leverage than when each party plays against the other.

Pooling resources to get an advantage works well in the business world. For instance, a partnership faced significant changes in the marketplace. The relationship was not financially sustainable going forward for the service provider. Having negotiated a deal in early 2009, the financial levers for the deal were no longer valid, causing the service provider to lose money. Nevertheless, the buying company told the service provider repeatedly that it did not know if it was getting the "best deal," so would have to put the work out to bid. Normally, that would be the end of the story.

When the service provider suggested during a senior leadership meeting that it would not compete on the work because it was losing money on the account, the tone of the conversations changed for the better. The buying company could no longer use the threat of the RFP (request for proposal) to rein in the service provider. The service provider genuinely exposed a financial flaw in the relationship that would have plagued all other partners.

This is yet another way that the principles of autonomy and loyalty work together for the benefit of the relationship. It is each company's obligation to make decisions for its own benefit, while also staying loyal to the partnership. After all, the buying company was simply making hollow threats. It did not have a sincere intention to transition the work; it needed a prod to get real.

### *Leverage the Six Guiding Principles*
In traditional negotiation theory, there are three forms of leverage: *positive*, having what the other side wants or needs, *negative*, threats of sanction, and *normative*, using shared norms or principles to promote the arguments. Nearly all negotiators know about positive and negative

leverage. But few have even heard about normative leverage, let alone used it effectively. Yet that is what Getting to We is all about: leveraging the shared principles for the benefit of the partnership.

Normative leverage uses the guiding principles to the partnership's advantage. Let's say that when it comes time to assess risk, business unit leaders agree on a plan to allocate and mitigate risk. Then, without the knowledge of the business units, the legal team takes a hard-line approach during the negotiation that shifts risk to the service provider.

A normative argument would leverage the principles of integrity, loyalty, and honesty. Loyalty to the relationship, when combined with honesty and autonomy, would dictate that the parties should have a risk allocation conversation. The principle of integrity means acting consistently with the principles all the time, not just when it is convenient.

Therefore, the legal team would work with the business unit leaders to understand the risk allocation and mitigation plan and then act accordingly in the best interests of the partnership.

### Honesty Is the Only Policy

Earlier in the Getting to We process, the parties agreed to honesty as one of the six guiding principles. Basically, when parties commit to be honest, they agree to tell the truth, both about facts in the world and about their intentions and experiences of those facts. People have also committed to having accurate and authentic conversations with each other. Therefore, honesty is really the only policy, and all forms of dishonesty as negotiation tactics must be avoided.

Bluffing is the most widespread tactic and the opposite of an accurate and authentic conversation. In fact, bluffing is so prevalent that rather than setting the expectation of honesty, negotiators would rather learn how to read body language to detect the lie. A bluff is most often an exaggeration that is somewhat meaningful, but not fraudulent. For example, negotiators will bluff about the viability of their BATNA's. What makes the bluff so effective is its elusiveness. Generally, there is no way of fact-checking the bluff.

Bluffing is a damaging tactic, but people find it difficult to give up. People say, "If I'm not going to get caught bluffing and everyone else does it, why be honest? I'd be giving up my advantage." In the situation above where the company wasn't sure that it was getting a good deal, the service provider quite literally called the company's bluff. It did so not to gain an advantage, but rather to be honest about the state of relationship.

Bluffing and similar tactics erode trust. As trust fades, so does adherence to other principles. People think, "If I don't trust you, I'll justify my own dishonesty. If I'm dishonest with you, and you find out, you'll think twice about reciprocating when it is your turn." Thus starts a downward spiral in the relationship.

Bluffing is not the only form of lying that severely damages trust. The sincere little white lies people tell each other are equally corrosive. Companies ought to encourage a policy of honesty under all circumstances.

People usually justify telling white lies. First, they have the sincere intention not to hurt another person. Second, the excuse might be that "it wasn't about anything important." Well, that is a matter of perspective. At a meeting between a buying company and its service provider, the sparks flew as the subject of telling each other little white lies came up. In the final analysis, sincere intentions do not matter; actions do. As people become aware of the little white lies, trust declines and resentments build.

It is imperative that companies do not let small acts of dishonesty creep into a relationship. Dan Ariely warns in a recent book, *The (Honest) Truth About Dishonesty: How We Lie to Everyone—Especially Ourselves*,[8] that dishonesty can easily become a social norm and spread throughout an organization. If dishonesty is not curbed early, it can lead to a series of negative tit-for-tat actions that can ultimately destroy a relationship.

### Leave Money on the Table

Many, many articles and books discuss various concession tactics, all from a WIIFMe point of view. The authors of these works describe ways to get the most out of the other guy without giving up too much. That is fine in a purely transactional situation. Partnerships depend on reciprocity, however.

Reciprocity fuels the relationship, both in good and in bad ways. As noted in chapter 2, Nobel laureate Oliver Williamson suggested that companies "leave money on the table."[9] Williamson notes that leaving money on the table is an act of trustworthiness. Rather than triggering a downward spiral, partners want to trigger a cycle of generosity. Leaving some money on the table fosters that cycle of increasing generosity.

Parties genuinely want the other side to go out of its way to meet the vision and the goals. During a recent series of negotiations between a large multinational company and its service provider, discussions about cost reductions became heated. The service provider's representatives became agitated at what they perceived to be unrealistic cost reduction demands that would either impact service levels or diminish profitability.

The service provider's negotiators left the room. When they came back, the company's representatives spontaneously said, "We have pushed you guys too far—you are right. We'll pay the higher rate for this because we don't want to put your profitability in jeopardy."[10] The service provider has told that story to its employees many times and always with the same message: let's look for ways to be generous for the sake of the partnership. The customer's decision to leave money on the table, in the service provider's opinion, was an act of generosity. A generous act has the power to escalate into a series of more good acts.

### Shared Vision, Shared Agenda

In a highly collaborative relationship, the parties are working toward a shared vision, as described in chapter 4. That shared vision continues to guide the parties even to the point of setting agendas for meetings. Furthermore, the principle of loyalty means that the relationship is its own entity, and therefore the partnership has its own agenda. This means that when living the We philosophy in the daily, monthly, quarterly, and annual meetings, agendas are built by contributions from all stakeholders.

Procter & Gamble (P&G) and Jones Lang LaSalle (JLL) are a good example. P&G wanted a partner who would take charge of P&G properties, not just take care of them.[11] That purpose has its own agenda items, irrespective of who places them on the agenda. Early on in the relationship of P&G and JLL the two parties met to discuss and approve transformation initiatives that JLL would work on. Unfortunately, as JLL reviewed the list, P&G employees were not enthusiastic about many of the ideas. On one particular topic P&G'ers exclaimed, "Oh, we've thought of that before...it will be too hard to do!" Bill Thummel, JLL chief operating officer-corporate solutions, stood up and spoke out. Commanding attention, but with a grin, he said, "You say you want innovation, but you won't accept change!"

William Reeves, corporate real estate leader for P&G, instantly stood up to offer a direct, simple response. "You are right. And that is precisely what we do not want to do."

The entire team went back to every item on the agenda and carefully considered each item. P&G changed its attitude by thoughtfully re-evaluating the transformative processes JLL brought to the partnership. Those processes generated many successes, including saving P&G millions of dollars and twice earning JLL P&G's Supplier of the Year award.

Many mediators apply the following principle when resolving a dispute: the person who puts an issue on the discussion agenda is the only person who can take that item off the agenda. This works well for two reasons. First, each person gets a say on the pressing issues regardless of rank or power. Second, it weeds out issues that are red herrings. Since all issues will be discussed, people are reluctant to put up a false issue. It doesn't look good when someone puts an issue up for discussion and then declines to discuss it. This process also balances power between the parties by allowing everyone to place issues on the agenda.

### Avoid Opportunism

Focusing on interests is different in a WIIFMe world than in a WIIFWe world. In the WIIFMe world, negotiators listen to take advantage first and seek mutual gain second. In other words, negotiators will only give something (a trade-off or a concession) if they have no other option. Many negotiation authors have tried to soften the excesses of the WIIFMe mentality by instructing negotiators to focus on the other party's interests in order to evaluate whether they have anything to offer in exchange for something they want. The focus on interests in the WIIFMe mindset is about finding out how the parties can find a positive answer to the question "what's in it for me?"

The WIIFMe mentality feeds a destructive problem at the bargaining table—opportunism. In chapter 1 opportunism is defined as the desire and the ability to take advantage of someone because you can. Unfortunately, many companies don't view opportunism as a bad thing when negotiating with their partner, and negotiators have developed ways to exploit or defend against acts of opportunism.

When entering the WIIFWe world, the old concepts and views no longer apply. The parties now form a joint entity *with its own interests*. The parties will, of course, still think of their own interests, but they ensure that what is in their own best interest is also in the best interest of the joint entity. There is no room for opportunism.

## READY TO TALK ABOUT MONEY?

At this point in the process negotiators reading this may scratch their heads, wondering when they will finally get to talk about money. After all, "show me the money" is a topic that dominates many business negotiations. Well, the time has finally come. Now that the parties have agreed to negotiate using rules, strategies, tactics, and a style that will support a highly collaborative relationship, they are ready to face the challenge of negotiating money. The next chapter outlines a value exchange model that drives long-term mutual gain.

# CHAPTER 8

# NEGOTIATING MONEY FOR MUTUAL BENEFIT

The rubber hits the road when negotiating money and allocating risks and rewards. The value potential from collaboration is *the* reason why companies establish commercial relationships. Without an expectation of long-term mutual gain, companies would be better off negotiating traditional transaction-based relationships centered on achieving only self-serving goals.

Often, parties entering into highly collaborative relationships know there is more value—usually latent value—by working together. But, they do not know how to unleash that value in a highly collaborative relationship. In a truly collaborative partnership, *value is created and allocated in a continuous process for mutual gain by making balanced exchanges.* We call this the Creative Value Allocation process.

This chapter provides a vital framework to help parties negotiate the creation and allocation of value, risks, and rewards for long-term mutual benefit by making balanced value exchanges. It does not outline the pros and cons of various pricing mechanisms, such as fixed-fee or cost-plus. There are other resources that offer this type of guidance.[1] The process of creating and allocating value goes beyond traditional efforts to expand the pie, and therefore it is worthwhile to take a critical look at those efforts and how those efforts differ from a WIIFWe approach.

## THE UNDERLYING PHILOSOPHY OF VALUE ALLOCATION

There are two dimensions of value that must be considered to optimize value between parties: value creation and value sharing. Value creation is straightforward. In the context of negotiating value for maximum benefit, business people are told the same things: expand the pie before dividing it, find options for mutual gains, spend time to create value before starting to claim a share of the value. That way each partner can unlock potential value: more pie.

The underlying WIIFWe mindset distinguishes creating value from the more traditional ways that business people negotiate value. Highly collaborative relationships constantly look for opportunities to create value by making investments and/or introducing various innovations to the relationship. Highly collaborative partnerships cannot afford to end up in the classic trap of negotiating a *price* for a transaction. Rather, they focus on sharing value as it is created at various stages of the relationship.

## WHAT IS VALUE?

Value is the regard people hold for something. People often place a value relative to the worth, merit, and/or utility of something, whether tangible or nontangible. Value has both objective and subjective characteristics. Subjectively, value is about expectations, preferences, and tastes, for example. Objectively, value can be defined in a more tangible form as increased benefits and opportunities and decreased costs and risks.

*Value is relative.* Organizations and individuals often place a different value on the same thing, whether a deadline, performance metric, or item. The difference of value gives negotiators much room to develop creative solutions. Business people approach negotiating value in three ways. Each approach has its own attributes.

## THREE WAYS TO NEGOTIATE VALUE

There are three primary ways to negotiate value. In this section each of these ways is explored; we show how organizations can approach pie expansion and pie sharing using the classic orange story in the book *Getting to Yes,*[2] referred to in chapter 1. The moral of this story is to look at underlying interests to divide the orange between two people who have different reasons for wanting the orange. Conventional best practice as advocated in *Getting to Yes* is to not fight over who will get more of the orange, but to seek to understand the other party's interest. The moral of the story goes that a win-win is if one party gets the pulp and the other gets the peel. While this is indeed a "win-win," the story is, however, still only a story on how to get to yes, not on how to get to We. The Creative Value Allocation process provides a path to get beyond yes and get to We. The following section is devoted to explaining the primary ways that organizations create and distribute value using the orange story.

## Value Exchange/Value Claiming

Most organizations use a conventional transaction-based approach for exchaging value. Conversations center mostly around determining a price and shifting risk. *Value exchange* is the process of exchanging resources. Referring to the orange story to demonstrate, let's say that Bob and Annie are business colleagues discussing what to do with the orange. Bob wants the pulp for his company while Annie wants the peel for hers.

If the pulp has a value of $1.00 to Bob's company and the peel has a value of $1.00 for Annie's company, the total value of the orange is $2.00. Annie has an orange and Bob has $1. Bob approaches Annie and asks if she would be willing to sell her orange for $1.00. Annie agrees that $1 is an equitable amount and she exchanges her orange for Bob's $1.00.

*Value claiming* is the process of attempting to get the largest share of a limited resource, such as money, raw materials, time or even a single orange. Claiming existing value is a win-lose mentality; it is also the most limiting negotiation method. In fact, some companies take it so far that they abuse their power to extract value from the other party (i.e., I want the orange, but I am only going to pay 50 cents.).

Unfortunately, most negotiation books and most negotiators focus almost exclusively on the strategies and tactics for exchanging and claiming value. For example, there are many strategies and tactics for negotiating price and price increases, costs, penalties and incentives, limitations of liability and indemnification clauses.[3] Looking back at the orange story, if Bob and Annie used conventional negotiation tactics, they would discuss ways to split the orange. Each company would get some pulp and some peel even though Bob's company wants all the pulp and Annie's company all the peel.

But by dividing the orange in half, each getting half the pulp and peel, Bob's company and Annie's company will each get only 50 cents in value. The total deal value is then only $1.00, half of the potential value of $2.00 had they met each other's needs. Moreover, when trapped in zero-sum thinking, negotiators make some common mistakes that restrict the parties from getting the full potential out of the orange.

Bob and Annie's negotiation represents the typical price conversations that dominate customer/service provider relationships. The service provider responds to a request for proposal with a price. The buying company enters negotiations by demanding a much lower price before it can award the business to the supplier. Each company will do its best to claim as much value as possible and go back and forth until a deal is struck. The company with the most relative bargaining power will claim the most value; value is extracted from the company with the least power.

## Creating Value and then Claiming Value

The second—and better—way that business people negotiate value is by *creating value and then claiming value.* Business scholars tell negotiators that to create value or to expand the pie, the parties must take a more collaborative approach, showing trust and transparency and an attitude of joint problem solving. Value creation combines cooperative techniques to expand the pie. The goal is to push the value to the fullest extent possible, to the place that maximizes both companies' outcomes without decreasing the outcomes of either partner before splitting up the value.[4] Once value is created, organizations focus on claiming their portion of the value.

Refering to the orange story, if Bob and Annie maximized the value of the orange, Bob's company would get all of the pulp and Annie's company would get all of the peel. During discussions about the orange, Bob and Annie discuss each other's interests, and decide that Bob's company will get the pulp and Annie's company the peel. They've unleashed the latent value—expanded the pie—and divided it to meet their respective needs. Each company has maximized the total value of $2.00. In this example, they have created as much value from the single orange as possible by looking at their underlying interests for wanting the orange.

That seems simple enough. Yet many companies don't reach their potential of $1.00 each for their share of the orange. Why not? In all likelihood, Bob and Annie undervalue their partner's needs and overvalue their needs. They end up trapping themselves in a zero-sum game.

Conventional "gain-sharing" illustrates how companies first create value then claim it. In theory, gain-sharing should work just fine. The premise of typical gain-sharing is for a buying company to pay a service provider a portion of any cost savings achieved from the service provider's efforts. In reality, many service providers report their clients often succumb to opportunism and typically don't make gain-share payments when it comes time for the service provider to claim its share of the value. Common excuses buying companies use are: "We gave you that idea" or "You can't prove your idea resulted in those savings." Regardless of the reasons, the typical approach to gain-sharing is fraught with frustration and disapointment.

A key flaw in the approach to first create value and then claim value is that companies and individuals tend to look only to their own self-interest when claiming value. They calculate how much they have versus what their counterpart has and make a judgment call regarding whether what they have is enough. It is awkward and unproductive to use a collaborative value creation process at the same time as a competitive value-claiming technique. Research shows that when negotiators use the competitive mentality for creating and then distributing value, they get less than optimal outcomes.[5] It is not surprising that many negotiators feel a tension between trying to be collaborative on the one hand (while creating value) and using competitive techniques (while claiming value) on the other hand. This tension is completely avoidable by approaching negoations with a WIIFWe mindset and a Getting to We process.

## Create Value and Devise Value Sharing Mechanisms for Mutual Gain

The third—and best—way that people negotiate value is to create value and then devise value sharing mechanisms for long-term mutual benefit.

We refer to this as Creative Value Allocation. The six principles outlined in chapter 5 guide conversations between individuals and organizations, and provide the collaborative foundation to create value and allocate value. Moreover, since partners now embrace the WIIFWe mindset, they develop a fair and balanced value allocation framework that can be used to create a pricing model, rather than establish a price.

Creative Value Allocation replaces the competitive tension associated with claiming value with a collaborative value allocation process. If Bob's company and Annie's company embraced the WIIFWe mindset they could actively discuss ways they could work together to get more oranges, not just determine how to find latent value in the one single orange. For example, Annie might recommend that she and Bob invest their time and resources to plant an orange tree. This decision would create a great deal of value for both companies, since they would be working together to care for the tree and benefit from the harvest, rather than haggle over one orange. However it could also pose a risk—what if the tree dies?—that the parties would need to share.

Using the Creative Value Allocation process, Bob and Annie would ponder the considerable planning, effort, financial investment and risks it takes to plant a tree. Bob and Annie would then develop a collaborative process for tracking the investments (buy the land and the seedling, water, fertilizer, and the labor to tend to the tree and to harvest the fruit) and then divide the fruit in proportion to each partner's contribution. Bob and Annie would create value and then allocate that value in an equitable manner throughout the duration of the relationship.

Companies that are committed to the WIIFWe mindset *should* use the Creative Value Allocation process; those choosing to adopt a Vested business model *must* adopt a Creative Value Allocation process that is supported by a pricing model with incentives that align the success of each party to the relationship. Agreeing to use Creative Value Allocation establishes a foundation for the parties to make fair and balanced exchanges throughout the duration of the relationship—something that is crucial because of the dynamic nature of business.

The rest of this chapter outlines the Creative Value Allocation Process. To begin, there are different types of value to create and allocate.

## FOUR VALUE CHIPS

In a We relationship, *value for the partnership is created by exchanging four types of "value chips."* There are four general kinds of value-creating actions that parties can exchange. These are:

- increased benefits
- decreased costs
- increased opportunities
- decreased risks

Each of these four actions represents one value chip that companies exchange with each other. When exchanges are made, value is simultaneously *created and allocated* between the parties. Let's look at the four categories of value chips.

### Increased Benefits

People create value when they create benefits for one another. There are numerous ways to create benefits. A service provider can create benefits for a buying company by providing more services or services of better quality, by improving the company's brand, by increasing the company's turnover of goods, and so on. The company, in turn, can create benefits by paying more to the service provider for its services, by awarding it extended contract terms, by increasing the scope of work, and so on.

For example, assume that a bank that is competing for customers in a tight marketplace places a high value on programs that increase customer loyalty. Those programs can range from teller services, to credit card application processing, to call center response times. If these programs increase customer loyalty there is both monetary and nonmonetary benefits, i.e. value to the bank.

### Decreased Costs

Value is also created when a party can decrease costs for another party. Costs are constraints that could prevent a partner from achieving its goals. If costs decrease, constraints are removed and value increases.

To continue the example above, if the call center not only increases customer loyalty but also takes measures to operate in more cost efficient ways, (and the call center passes cost savings on to the bank) value is created for the bank in the form of decreased costs. On the other hand, the bank can reduce the call center's costs by allowing it to staff the center based on predictable call volume forcasts rather than directing it to have a minimum number of staff members at any given time.

## Increased Opportunities

Value can also be created if a party generates increased *opportunities* for another party. An opportunity is the possibility that something positive will happen. A company can, for example, increase the opportunities for a service provider by providing it with an option for an extended contract term if the service provider hits certain pre-defined targets or outcomes. In fact, many forms of positive incentives in commercial relationships are examples of value creation by increasing opportunities. The value of an opportunity depends on the degree of the positive impact of the benefit and the likelihood of realization of the opportunity.

## Decreased Risk

Finally, value is created when a party decreases risks for another party. A risk is the possibility that something negative will happen. The value of the risk thus depends on the degree of negative impact if the risk materializes and the likelihood of the risk materializing. Some risks are out of the parties' control; some are within their control. Typical examples of risks that are out of the parties' control include increased prices for raw materials, foreign currency exchange risks, and decreased demand for the product or service. Risks that are within partners' control include predictable delays from organizational misalignment, inaccuracies in reporting, and poor talent management.

## BALANCED EXCHANGES

Creating value by exchanging value chips must be fair and balanced for all parties. One partner may decrease costs while the other partner may

Figure 8.1   Balanced exchange

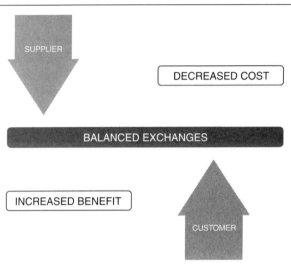

receive increased benefits or decreased risks. Figure 8.1 illustrates this concept.

It is not possible to look at creating value from one partner's perspective. Decreased costs will come at the expense of one partner if not properly compensated in an exchange of value. For example, if a buying company unilaterally forces a service provider to decrease costs, value is created for the buying company, and not for the relationship, because the decreased costs of the company is offset by decreased benefits (for example, lowered margins) for the service provider. Thus, decreased costs for the company (in this example) will only create value for the partnership if the service provider gets something in return, such as increased benefits in the form of an incentive. Figure 8.2 demonstrates this unbalanced exchange.

*Exchange*, guided by the principle of reciprocity, is the key to creating value for the partnership. This is not a traditional zero-sum game since each party always gets something in return. In the process of creating value, the partners ask themselves what they want and what they can provide in return for what they want. They will then discuss those wants and needs and make all necessary exchanges to best achieve the shared vision. As parties discuss the ways the partnership can meet its goals, parties will look for opportunities to exchange one type of value for another, always aiming for a fair exchange.

Figure 8.2   Unbalanced exchange

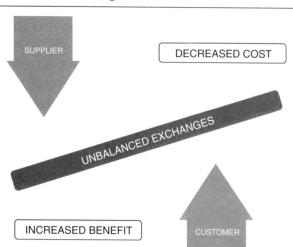

Some business people wonder if a balanced exchange is the same as an exact exchange of value ($100 of value in exchange for $100 in value, for instance). A balanced value exchange is not the same as an exact exchange of value. Balanced exchanges rely on people's perception of the relative value of what is being exchanged. Each party gives something it perceives as being less valuable and it gets something it perceives as more valuable in return. Partners create value by making exchanges that further their shared vision and goals. So long as both parties are genuinely satisified with the exchange and the partnership is enhanced.

For example, a service provide might introcduce a piece of technology that inhances security at its customer's building. The service provider's customer might place a high value on security even though the technology might not have been costly to implement. Each partner places a value on the technology that is not an exact dollar for dollar exchange, yet both benefit from the exchange.

## NINE EXAMPLES OF THE CREATIVE VALUE ALLOCATION PROCESS

There are innumerous ways that value can be created and allocated by exchanging value chips. If single exchanges of one value chip for another value chip are considered, sixteen possibilities exist, as shown in figure 8.3.

Figure 8.3    Value exchanges

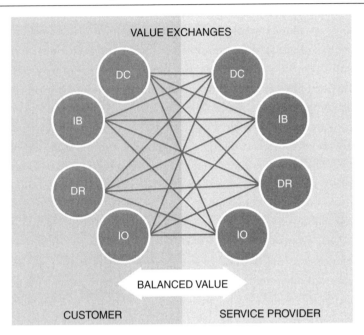

Each circle represents one value chip. For example, the parties can exchange decreased costs (DC) for decreased costs (DC). Each line represents a potential two-way exchange between the parties. Below are nine examples of two-way value creation by exchanging one value chip for another value chip.

## Company Seeks Increased Benefits in Exchange for Service Provider Receiving Increased Benefits (IB-IB)

Many companies seeking process improvements (e.g., efficiencies gained through automation or applying lean or Six Sigma techniques) look for opportunities to increase their benefits as a result of process improvements. For example, a buying company awarded a service provider a contract to handle a number of the buying company's financial processes. The work included using software developed over the years by the company's employees. The company knew that the software needed improvements because it caused errors to the financial processes from time to time. The company wanted better software (increased benefits and decreased risks) since improved software quality would speed up the financial processes and make the buying company more reliable.

The partners discussed how to motivate the service provider to continuously improve the software's performance. The partners, who had a great deal of mutual trust, opted for a very simple solution. The service provider provided the buying company with an appointed quality manager. The manager found bugs in the software, analyzed how those bugs affected the company's financial processes, and then implemented corrective measures. While the company got the benefit of improved software, the service provider got the benefit of increased margins as a result of the additional scope of the contract.

It is noteworthy that not all exchanges of increased scope of work for additional payment create value. The partners' expectations play an important role here. Many buying companys contract with a service provider with the main purpose of decreasing costs. In a typical WIIFMe arrangement, the service provider may offer low prices for the work requested, but still the costs end up being much higher for the company than budgeted. What often happens is that the company is only expecting to pay for the work specified in the contract. If the company has failed to specify all work that is needed to achieve the buying company's goals, the company will have to order additional work from the service provider and pay for that. It is not uncommon that this is also a bet that the service provider has made when offering the low prices. Because of information asymmetries, i.e. the supplier's better knowledge of the needed scope of work, the service provider can compensate for the low prices on the requested work with increased scope of work.

Although an exchange of benefits (the additional work in exchange for money) is made, value is not necessarily created in this last partnership example. Value, as noted above, also has subjective characteristics. If the additional work and the corresponding increased costs were not anticipated by the buying company, the latter will not consider the additional work as a benefit but as a disappointment of its expectations.

So, increased benefits that are unexpected are not necessarily valuable. This emphasizes the importance of constant information transparency, following the principles of autonomy and loyalty.

## Company Seeks Increased Benefits in Exchange for Service Provider Receiving Increased Opportunities (IB-IO)

Some buying companies recognize that in order to get increased benefits, either the company or the service provider has to make a commitment to invest. When the service provider chooses to make the investment, it can exchange its investment for increased opportunities.

For example, a manufacturer wanted to improve a costly process that was not core to its business. It partnered with a service provider in the industry that took over the process, making it much more efficient and effective (increasing benefits and decreasing costs). In order to meet the manufacturer's strict timelines, though, the service provider needed to make some expensive capital investments at its facility. The upside of those capital investments was increased capacity at the service provider's facility. The service provider sold the excess capacity to its other customers, thus increasing its opportunities and ultimately its benefits too.

Buying companies often stand in the way of service providers' realizing increased opportunities by restricting service providers from exploiting their investments. Good examples are when buying companies insist they own any intellectual property as a result of process improvements, or they contractually restrict the service provider in other ways from capitalizing on its investment. Buying companies justify their position, stating they paid for the improvements. This is a conventional value-claiming argument that will not yield increased benefits through suppliers' investments because it is a one-sided benefit for the buying company.

## Company Receives Increased Benefits in Exchange for Service Provider Receiving Decreased Costs (IB-DC)

This scenario is much less common. Buying companies are attracted to the idea but often fail to follow through. In order for buying companies to get increased benefits while also reducing the service provider's costs, the parties must think in terms of innovation, transformation, and change management. For example, a company outsourced a noncore function "as is", also commonly known as a "lift and shift." The buying company was attracted to the service provider's best practices because of the service provider's potential efficiencies. Unfortunately, the buying company was completely unwilling to make internal changes to accommodate the service provider's best practices. As a result, the service provider was stuck performing tasks that actually cost money.

If the buying company truly wanted the increased benefits from leveraging the service providers's best practices, the buying company would have to implement change management strategies. This is not easy. Nevertheless, if buying companies choose this exchange of values, then they have to be willing to do what is necessary within their own organization so that the service provider can decrease its costs and improve its margins.

## Company Receives Decreased Costs in Exchange for Service Provider Receiving Increased Benefits (DC-IB)

Cost reduction is one of the main drivers behind many companies' decisions to allow a service provider to produce goods or perform a service traditionally produced or performed in-house. While companies also seek shortened time to market, increased availability of the latest technology, etc., cost reduction will probably always remain an important driver. A company that wants lowered costs while applying a WIIFWe approach has to ask itself, "What can we provide in return for such lowered costs?"

There is not an obvious answer to this question. Lowered costs are too often obtained by unilateral use of coercion. Companies with bargaining power often take the approach that a service provider should lower its prices or increase efficiency out of pure gratitude for being allowed to stay on as a service provider. That approach—WIIFMe—may work when buying simple commodities. But in long-term, collaborative partnerships another approach is needed. Decreased costs will not be obtained without giving something in return.

Buying companies can offer service providers many benefits in exchange for getting lower costs. Some service providers have received the following: increased volume, guaranteed volume floors, or additional work, for example. For obvious reasons, service providers prefer to receive tangible benefits in exchange for tangible cost reductions. It is not a mutual exchange to offer promises such as the ability to bid on future products, revisit pricing in the middle of the contract cycle, or referrals to other business units that might need the service provider's services. Those are shadow trade-offs. The actual benefits lurk in the shadows and rarely come to fruition even though the company receives real cost savings.

## Company Receives Decreased Costs in Exchange for Service Provider Receiving Decreased Costs (DC-DC)

Exchanging decreased costs for decreased costs can get complicated. It often takes a fair bit of transparency to uncover the cost drivers and then analyze the risks associated with them.

For example, a company wanted lower costs associated with payroll services. The payroll service provider's service delivery consisted of day-to-day payroll administration using a number of information technology tools. Some of these tools were the service provider's property, while others were licensed from third-party suppliers. The service provider incurred license fees and overhead costs because it managed the third-party relationships without adequate compensation, thus decreasing the service provider's margin.

After a discussion on how to meet the buying company's desire for a cost decrease, the parties realized the third-party licenses and their management were driving up the service provider's costs. The company agreed that it could manage its relationship with the third-party providers more efficiently and at lower costs than the service provider could. They agreed to allocate those relationships to the company instead. As a result, the service provider's costs decreased. And although the company faced some additional costs for managing the third-party suppliers, the price decrease from the service provider exceeded these additional costs. Thus, the company got its required cost decrease in exchange for a cost decrease for the service provider too.

## Company Receives Decreased Cost in Exchange for Service Provider Receiving Decreased Risk (DC-DR)

Decreased costs can also be obtained in return for decreased risks. There are several good examples of such exchanges. For instance, a company selling goods or services usually includes the value of risk in its pricing, referred to as "risk premiums." When partners are transparent not only about costs, but also about the associated risks inherent in the performance of the work, they can find solutions to decrease prices that are based on reducing the supplier's risk.

A small chemical company successfully decreased its costs while also reducing the service provider's risk. The chemical company outsourced its warehouse logistics. In the first five years of the agreement, the chemical company demanded excessive insurance coverage, high limits on the service provider's liability and strict indemnification provisions. The service provider passed the costs of those provisions on to the chemical company. There were no safety incidents in that first five year term, but the service provider kept the price premium the chemical company paid for the insurance coverange and limitations on liability, etc.

When the chemical company and the service provider negotiated the next five years of their agreement, they embraced the WIIFWe mindset. Decreased costs and risks were in the best interest of the relationship. The chemical company became self insured and also took responsibility to train all the service provider's employees. The service provider dramatically reduced its costs and passed the savings on to the chemical company. Warehouse safety also improved. This is a good example of the principle of loyalty in action. The parties put the partnership's interests first and found a solution that also met their needs.

## Company Receives Decreased Costs in Exchange for Service Provider Receiving Increased Opportunities (DC-IO)

Buying companies can decrease costs in exchange for offering the service provider increased opportunities. Typically, companies that enter this type of exchange are looking to maximize some process improvement or innovation.

An example of a successful exchange of decreased costs for increased opportunities involved a construction general contractor (GC) that used a specialized subcontractor for a large government project. The GC planned to bid for a large construction project and knew it would need the subcontractor to perform the work. The GC also needed the subcontractor to decrease its prices for the GC to win the contract. The subcontractor agreed to decrease its prices and in return obtained the increased opportunity for higher volumes of work associated with the project should the GC win the construction contract—which it did.

## Company Receives Increased Opportunity in Exchange for the Service Provider's Receiving Increased Opportunity (IO-IO )

There are some questions that are asked more and more frequently by companies and organizations around the world: How can we innovate? How can we have a partnership that promotes innovation? How can we find the best-in-class partners in their respective fields and incentivize them to assist us in strengthening our market position through innovation? The common theme here is, of course, *innovation*.

To ask for innovation is to ask for increased opportunities. Since to innovate is to find *new* ways of doing things, it is hard to predict the results. Contracting for innovation is therefore contracting for the possibility of benefits—for opportunities.

A technology company worked with a facilities management service provider to manage its data centers. Both companies were frustrated by the time and effort it took for them to gather important data. They worked together to find a solution that was in the best interest of the partnership.

They undertook a project to develop a piece of software to customize the service provider's existing reporting software. The technology company combined its specialized knowledge with the service provider's existing product to improve reporting and the management of the data centers. They each took a gamble that the innovation would pay off, and it did. More important, the technology company agreed that the service provider could market the enhaced reporting software to cusomters that did not compete with the technology company.

## Company Receives Decreased Risk in Exchange for Service Provider Receiving Decreased Risk (DR – DR)

Another way for parties to create value is to take measures to decrease each other's risks. The often used "earn-out price clause" is a good example of the exchange of decreased risks. Companies often use this mechanism when they have different estimates of future economic returns from a company or another asset for sale. For example, the seller predicts that the net profit of its company will increase by 10 percent every year the coming five years. The seller will then ask for a purchase price reflecting this profit potential.

A buyer is usually more hesitant and estimates that the profit increase will, at best, be 5 percent per year over five years, which results in a lower valuation of the company. Neither party wants to take the risk that the other party's forecast is right.

Using an earn-out clause, the parties agree that the buyer will pay a small sum of money when the deal is closed and the additional purchase price is based on the *actual net profit* of the purchased company. In such a situation, the buyer's risk of paying too high a price is decreased, and the seller's risk of receiving too little money for the company is likewise decreased.

## Other Forms of Value Exchanges

The above discussion offers a framework for allocating risk and reward in a fair and balanced manner. Nine forms of two-way exchanges were identified, using the concept of value chips. In reality, nothing says that only two-way exchanges—changing one-for-one—need be made. It is possible that parties will make multiple exchanges. For example, a company can obtain increased benefits *and* decreased costs in exchange for increased benefits in the form of incentive programs for the supplier. The number of possible exchanges and combinations of exchanges is extensive.

> **Topics for Discussion**
>
> - Who will need to be a part of the Creative Value Allocation process? (Think in terms of people who can evaluate the value created by the balanced exchange, not just the person who can agree to a price.)
> - What preparatory work is needed to have a thoughtful Creative Value Allocation conversation?
> - What mechanisms are needed to verify the value that's been created? (Measure decreased costs or increased benefits, for example.)
> - What individuals with each company can best evaluate the value of something to the partnership?
> - How will those people go about building a business case to evaluate the benefits of an innovation to the partnership?

## THE GUIDING PRINCIPLES OF CREATIVE
## VALUE ALLOCATION

The Creative Value Allocation process is a general framework that can be applied to relationships no matter the size, complexity or industry. Companies must agree together to use this framework to promote the achievement of their shared vision. All Creative Value Allocation processes have one important element in common: they are created by and founded on the application of the guiding principles described in chapter 5. The guiding principles give the relationship the stability, flexibility, and agility it needs so that the parties can continue to create and allocate value during the lifetime of the relationship.

Creative Value Allocation builds on a core composed of the principles of reciprocity, loyalty, and equity. The other principles of autonomy, honesty, and integrity provide additional support.

Reciprocity lies at the heart of Creative Value Allocation. In fact, *without reciprocity little value can be created for the partnership.* In most situations when, as was noted earlier, a powerful company uses coercion to obtain a lower price from its service provider, no value is created since the powerful company gains at the expense of its service provider. Positive value can *only* be created *by* the *exchange* of value.

Reciprocity creates momentum in the value-creating process. We recognize this from other parts of our lives. If someone starts to exchange, for example, Christmas gifts or dinner invitations with someone else, both will feel obliged to continue the exchange process, even if they have exchanged the same number of gifts or dinner invitations. The reciprocity of the gift exchange rituals of society not only involves obligations to return in kind but also obligations to give in the first place.[6]

In the same way that reciprocity keeps gift exchanges going, reciprocity keeps the value creation process going in commercial and other negotiations and during the lifetime of the partnership. As long as the partners are governed by reciprocity, they will naturally continue to explore additional ways to create and allocate value for the partnership.

Reciprocity is, however, not enough for Creative Value Allocation. It is reciprocity in combination with the principles of loyalty and equity that creates an atmosphere encouraging a fair allocation mechanism. The principle of loyalty obliges the parties to consider the interests of the partnership as if it is a single entity. This means, as described earlier, that the parties focus on maximizing benefits and opportunities and minimizing costs and risks *to the partnership*.

Assume, for example, that a buying company and a service provider have jointly discovered potential opportunities to innovate and therefore improve the company's warehouse operations. Applying only the principle of loyalty likely will not result in realizing innovative opportunities because innovation involves risk. Innovation requires making investments, always in time and often also in money, without being certain of a positive outcome. Since loyalty requires risk minimization, loyalty alone will not promote innovation. If the company wants innovation, the partnership will have to apply the principle of equity as well.

Value received by one partner must also be *proportionate* to the value it provides to its partner. This is the principle of equity in action. The buying company must incentivize the service provider to take on the risks associated with innovation. To incentivize the service provider means that the service provider must be *rewarded* in proportion to the risks undertaken.

Even though reciprocity, loyalty, and equity are the most important principles of Creative Value Allocation, they need to be supported by the other guiding principles. True reciprocity is not possible unless the parties can make autonomous decisions. Without honesty, many opportunities for additional value creation will never present themselves. And without integrity, the momentum created by reciprocity will be lost since it is integrity that ensures that the parties keep up with the practices for creating value they have adopted.

## CREATIVE VALUE ALLOCATION IN ACTION

Chapter 6 briefly profiled the highly successful US Department of Energy (DOE) and Kaiser-Hill Company LLC (Kaiser-Hill), a joint venture between CH2M Hill and Kaiser Engineers, a collaboration that transformed the polluted Rocky Flats nuclear production facility into a public park and wildlife sanctuary.[7] The Rocky Flats Closure Project also provides a great deal of insight into how the parties created and allocated value, not only when the contract was negotiated but over the lifetime of the partnership.

To fully understand and appreciate how the DOE and Kaiser-Hill applied the Creative Value Allocation process, this section outlines the background and an overview of the actual pricing model from the Rocky Flats Closure Project. To be clear, the DOE and Kaiser-Hill created a fully Vested agreement. This chapter focuses on the various value chip exchanges each party made.[8]

## Background on the Rocky Flats Closure Project

In 1989, the Federal Bureau of Investigation, Justice Department, and Environmental Protection Agency began an investigation into the Rocky Flats nuclear production site involving alleged environmental crimes for handling and storing nuclear waste. In 1992 President George H. W. Bush ordered the closure of Rocky Flats. Total closure and cleanup of a nuclear production facility had never been accomplished anywhere. The official United States Department of Energy 1995 Baseline Environmental Management Report estimated that the closure and cleanup project could last up to 75 years and cost up to $37 billion.

Two different contractors had made little progress in the cleanup and had cost taxpayers almost a $1 billion a year between 1989 and 1995. On July 1, 1995, the DOE signed a five-year contract with Kaiser-Hill to manage the Rocky Flats cleanup and closure. Ten years later, the project came in a staggering $27 billion under initial budget projections and 65 years ahead of initial timeline projections.[9]

## High-Level Overview of the Pricing Model

DOE and Kaiser-Hill entered into a contract with a clearly defined shared vision and desired outcomes aimed at properly cleaning and closing the Rocky Flats nuclear site in a safe and cost-effective manner. The contract was a flexible framework. Following the initial five-year contract, the parties entered into a Vested agreement in 1999 aimed at highly rewarding Kaiser-Hill for achieving the shared vision and desired outcomes. The pricing model is presented in figure 8.4.

The contract—a first of its kind for the DOE—had significant incentives tied to worker safety, unquestioned quality, budget compliance, and reduction of the time needed to complete the project.[10] The basic Kaiser-Hill fee was structured as a cost plus fee-at-risk with incentives. The cost plus approach was critical because the true scope and costs of the work were truly unknown—they were, at best, guestimates. Creating

Figure 8.4    Rocky Flats Closure Project pricing model

| BASE | | | TARGET FREE | INCENTIVES |
| --- | --- | --- | --- | --- |
| COST PASS THROUGH | MINIMUM FEE | FEE AT RISK | | STRETCH INCENTIVES |
| Project costs were passed through | Minimum Management Fee 3.77% | 5.23% of Fee "at risk" | 9.0% (combined management fee and at risk fee) | 11.6% Maximum Fee |
| | | • Fees paid for achieving Performance Targets | | • Fees paid for exceeding Performance Target |
| | | • Penalties for missing Peformance Targets | | |
| | | • Cost Share (KH kept 30 cents for every $1 under target budget and lost 70 cents for every $1 over budget) | | |

incentives tied directly to Kaiser Hill's ability achieve the shared vision and desired outcomes aligned Kaiser-Hill's interests with the DOE and taxpayer interests. The essence of the agreement was Vested; the more successful Kaiser-Hill was at meeting the shared vision and desired outcomes, the more successful Kaiser-Hill would be.

Under the agreement Kaiser-Hill's profit was connected to the final cost the DOE paid. For example, the 1999 contract extension stated that, if total costs were between $3.963 billion and $4.163 billion, Kaiser-Hill would earn the target fee. If actual costs were lower than the target cost, Kaiser-Hill earned an additional 30 cents for every dollar less than $3.963 billion. If costs exceeded the target cost, Kaiser-Hill's fee was reduced by 30 cents.

Kaiser-Hill also financed its own performance and submitted vouchers for payment. Not only did Kaiser-Hill have a portion of its fee-at-risk tied to cost, it put up its own money to drive innovations with the hope of achieving incentive payments if it performed well.

Lastly, Kaiser-Hill voluntarily offered performance incentive payments to all employees, pledging 20 percent of profits to the Rocky Flats workers at project end. Kaiser-Hill firmly believed in the WIIFWe mindset and believed employees needed rewards too—specifically in their pocketbooks. And greater rewards for the workers at Rocky Flats would yield greater results for the DOE and in turn greater profitability for Kaiser-Hill. This was WIIFWe thinking in action and at its best.

## ANALYSIS OF THE ROCKY FLATS CREATIVE VALUE ALLOCATION

The Rocky Flats Closure contract represents a good example of Creative Value Allocation mechanisms in operation. The DOE and Kaiser-Hill achieved this success not only because they adopted a WIIFWe mindset, but also because they faithfully adhered to all five Vested rules. Simply applying the Getting to We process to get to a WIIFWe mindset is powerful, but it cannot alone provide the essential elements needed to achieve the levels of transformational success seen in the Rocky Flats case study.[11]

In the section that follows, various aspects of the Creative Value Allocation process used by the DOE and Kaiser-Hill are outlined. Specifically, several exchanges of value chips are examined.

### Decreased Risks for Decreased Risks

Before Kaiser-Hill won the cleanup contract, Rocky Flats had a track record of poor safety, including holding the dubious record of the worst industrial fire in the history of the United States. In 1994, Building 771 was called the "most dangerous building in America" in an *ABC News Nightline* broadcast.[12] Rocky Flats scored well below DOE and construction industry averages for safety metrics when Kaiser-Hill took over in 1995. The 12-month rolling average for Total Recordable Case rate (the number of occupation-related incidents requiring more than basic first aid) in July 1995 was 7.6, above the construction industry average of 6.4 and the contractually obligated 3.5. Another key safety measure—the Lost Workday Case rate (restricted days away from work)—was at 4.6 in July 1995, well above the construction industry average of 2.4 and the contract target of 2.0.[13]

By the end of the project, Kaiser-Hill reduced a backlog of 900 employee grievances to a mere handful. In safety measures, Kaiser-Hill completed 60-plus million hours of work with no life-threatening injuries or environmental releases. It improved the Total Recordable Case (TRC) safety rate from 7.6 to 0.9 per full-time equivalent employee. And the Lost Workday Case rate dropped from 4.6 to 0.2, some 75 percent below other DOE sites and well below the construction industry average of 2.4.[14] In fact, the rate was so low that Kaiser-Hill was able to get a $300,000 rebate from its insurance company for the superior safety record.[15]

Finally, Kaiser-Hill enjoyed a unique opportunity to decrease risks that most suppliers don't enjoy—recovering actual costs associated with DOE delays. In other words, suppliers face a performance risk if their performance is tied to the buying company's performance. Because Kaiser-Hill could recover actual costs for DOE delays, it felt assured that the DOE would do all it could to perform its obligations in a timely manner, thereby ensuring the project's success.

## Decreased Costs for Increased Benefits and Increased Opportunities

Kaiser-Hill was also incentivized to reduce the DOE's costs. Kaiser-Hill earned 30 cents for every dollar it saved the DOE over the baseline targets. The DOE paid millions of dollars in incentive fees to Kaiser-Hill in exchange for hundreds of millions of dollars in savings to the US taxpayer. In fact, the incentives almost tripled Kaiser-Hill's profit margins over the average profit margin the DOE paid other contractors (the average is 4.1 percent, and Kaiser-Hill ultimately earned 11.6 percent profit margins with most of the money coming from incentive payments tied achieving the shared vision and desired outcomes).

The ability to earn favorable profit margins (note that only 3.7 percent profit margin was guaranteed) was a main factor in the success of the Rocky Flats project and a significant reason why Kaiser-Hill was willing to make a big bet that it could innovate its way to success.

In addition, the contract allowed Kaiser-Hill to commercialize the innovations and patents it created as part of the project. The DOE encouraged Kaiser-Hill to leverage its intellectual property rights in the private market palce. Kaiser-Hill saw tremendous value in the form of increased opportunities by taking incentives unique to Rocky Flats to the private sector.

The Rocky Flats Closure Project is a terrific example of how the parties approached the Creative Value Allocation process, in which value-creating factors of increased benefits and opportunities and decreased costs and risks were involved. It is also a great example of how to plant that orange tree.

## PLANTING AN ORANGE TREE

Chapter 1 talked about planting an orange tree rather than creatively dividing one orange to extract value. The Rocky Flats Closure Project clearly demonstrates that when parties embrace the WIIFWe mindset and follow the path all the way to reach a Vested agreement, organizations can reap amazing rewards, like planting an orange tree rather than dividing a single orange.

In doing so, Kaiser-Hill was highly incentivized to invest in sowing the seed—for once it blossomed, the seed developed into ample fruit for the DOE and Kaiser-Hill to share. In short, Kaiser-Hill found it was far more productive to stop figuring out how to divide one single orange and start figuring out how to plant a tree. The results were more than 200 innovations that enabled Rocky Flats to close 65 years ahead of schedule and $30 billion under original projections.

The success of the Rocky Flats Closure Project did not happen magically. Rather, it was the result of two parties choosing to embrace a WIIFWe mindset and carefully craft an agreement that followed Vested's Five Rules. What applied to Rocky Flats can apply to all business partnerships. The power of WIIFWe thinking is real.

Many companies will find great success using the Creative Value Allocation process outlined in this chapter. Yet, some partnerships may not think it is enough. They'll reach for the impossible and plant an orange tree.

## JUST WHEN YOU THINK YOU'RE DONE

At this point most negotiators probably think they are done. The parties have agreed on the details of the deal and monetary issues are sorted out. But in the Getting to We process there is one more vital step—living as We. The next section provides guidance for a relationship management structure that follows the six guiding principles.

# LIVING AS WE

When organizations arrive at the last step in the Getting to We process, the relationship is transformed into a true partnership. The important details of the relationship are fleshed out. Most negotiators think they are done.

In this way relationship negotiations resemble movie romances. In a typical movie romance, there is tension and excitement as the relationship grows. Then the couple finally gets married at the end of the movie. Everyone is happy as the music begins and the credits roll. Movie goers get up from their seats and move on to the next thing. No one really wonders if the on-screen couple will be happy six months from now or what it will take for the on-screen couple to stay happy for years to come.

Negotiators can be like those moviegoers. They are focused on getting the deal done—caught up in the drama and excitement. Rarely do they think about the long-term relationship after an agreement is reached. As far as these dealmakers are concerned, their job is done, and it is time to move on to the next deal.

In reality, negotiators are not done. The techniques described thus far are not by themselves enough to *live* a WIIFWe mindset. This section provides valuable insight into living with as We.

Step 5 can be considered complete only once the parties have *designed and institutionalized* an effective governance structure for the relationship where everyone involved embraces and applies the principles to the working relationships with one another. Everyone touching the relationship has to abide by the principles, not just the team developing the deal. This is equally true for new partnerships, existing partnerships, external and internal partnerships.

Chapter 9 outlines the important factors parties should consider when developing their relationship management framework. It also looks at the role that the guiding principles play in enforcing collaborative behaviors.

Chapter 10 relates two powerful stories about the *power of living as We*. Each of the companies profiled in this chapter achieved extraordinary results by embracing a WIIFWe mindset and following the Getting to We process.

# CHAPTER 9

# STEP 5: RELATIONSHIP MANAGEMENT

People unfamiliar with working in highly collaborative relationships often find it easy to fall into the familiar tug-of-war mentality. Without a framework and mechanisms for managing the relationship and living the guiding principles the parties have established, it is easy for old habits to reassert themselves. A sound relationship management structure provides a set of cohesive policies, processes, and decision-making rights that encourage parties to continuously collaborate. Think of these as mechanisms that when in operation will help keep the relationship running at peak performance long after the parties have gotten to "yes" and signed their deal.

In complex business relationships the processes and mechanisms for managing a relationship are known as governance. Vested's Rule 5 calls for "an insight, not an oversight governance structure." *The Vested Outsourcing Manual*[1] outlines a comprehensive framework for managing complex business-to-business agreements. Fully Vested relationships include comprehensive governance with four elements: relationship management, transformation management, exit management, and special concerns, such as governmental and regulatory issues that apply to the relationship.[2] Partnerships that complete the Getting to We process typically focus on one element of governance—relationship management. This is not to say that the other elements are unimportant. Rather, less complex deals may not need transformation and exit management structures, but all relationships regardless of their complexity need effective management in order to elicit collaborative behaviors. Therefore, this chapter focuses on the critical success factors and mechanisms of sound relationship management.

## SUCCESSFULLLY LIVING AS WE

Three primary success factors are the sine qua non when developing a relationship management structure. The first success factor includes a firm commitment to *live* the guiding principles that were established in chapter 5. In the second success factor, the parties maintain the relationship without interruption. This is especially important for bringing new people up to speed who will participate in the relationship throughout its life. The third success factor involves adopting a "systems" mentality that will ensure that the parties keep the relationship in sync as "business happens." This is best done by documenting the actual mechanisms the parties will use to manage the relationship on a day-to-day, month-to-month, quarter-to-quarter, and year-to-year basis. Each of these success factors is discussed in more detail.

### Living the Guiding Principles

Organizations deciding to embrace a WIIFWe mindset for their relationship must make the decision to live the guiding principles as adopted from chapter 5. Each organization must be willing to compel their people to focus efforts on achieving the shared vision while continuing to apply *all of the guiding principles*. While the parties should follow all of the guiding principles all the time, integrity takes center stage at this point in the Getting to We process.

As related in chapter 5, the principle of integrity obliges consistency by the partners in their decision-making and in their actions. That is, thriving partnerships have a transparent and consistent process for making decisions that promotes fairness. Consistency in decision-making ensures consistency in results, which in turn promotes predictability. Additionally, by living with integrity, the partners can come to trust that they will work for each other and the relationship simultaneously, eliminating the need for self-protection tactics.

For example, the power of the principles played itself out shortly after a manufacturer finalized a complex deal with a service provider.

The partners agreed to collect and then share information, which was then compiled into a joint report. That report was used to calculate the service provider's incentive bonus. The parties lived the principles of honesty and loyalty by transparently collecting data and then jointly creating one report.

Unfortunately, the manufacturer made a series of errors, and when combined with the service provider's data, these reduced the service provider's incentive payment by $200,000, a not insignificant amount. The service provider brought the manufacturer's data entry errors to the manufacturer's attention with the anticipation of trust. Because the manufacturer was loyal to the partnership, and because it wanted honesty in every interaction, the manufacturer agreed to reexamine the numbers.

But this is not the end of the story. Once the manufacturer learned of the mistake, one of its executives wanted to deny the errors so that the manufacturer could keep the money. The manufacturer's account manager then went to bat for the integrity of the relationship, reminding the executive that reciprocity and loyalty are two-way streets. If the manufacturer was no longer loyal to the partnership, the service provider's trust would surely weaken, and the flow of reciprocity would come to a halt. It was not worth damaging a highly profitable multimillion dollar partnership for a mere $200,000. The example shows how all of the principles, but especially integrity, benefit everyone by putting the relationship before short-term interests.

Sometimes getting people within the partnership to abide by the principles is hard. For example, one supply chain executive responsible for global initiatives applies the same process and vigor in establishing a WIIFWe mindset with her internal stakeholders as she does with her outsourcing partners. This executive's concerns with integrity were primarily focused on other vice presidents. Many of her counterparts nodded their heads in agreement when she rolled out collaborative partnership agreements. But these same vice presidents continued to behave in the same conventional WIIFMe ways.

The outsourcing executive attacked the WIIFMe attitude by painting a picture. She mapped out the benefit to the entire organization division by division, showing each vice president that if they worked with her to actually embody a WIIFWe mindset for two highly collaborative partnerships, they would all benefit. She said, "These guys were glued to the screen. They could not believe it. In fact, at one point I lost their attention because they were so focused on the chart I was showing them." Once her vice presidents understood the strategic value the two outsourcing parties could bring the organization and to the end user (the consumer), they were convinced. They started to think more globally about how the outsourcing relationships contributed to the success of the larger organization.[3]

## Relationship Continuity

Some business partnerships can last for decades and therefore must have a relationship management framework that will endure significant external changes while motivating the right kind of behaviors. Relationship continuity is similar to *business continuity*, a term often used in risk management circles. When planning for business continuity, a company asks, "If a crisis, outage, or some other event happens that could threaten to put a stop to business, what parts of the business, at a minimum, *must* continue to operate?" The company then develops plans to ensure that core business operations continue despite the crisis. While similar in concept, relationship continuity is broader than business continuity. Relationship continuity is not only about what has to be done at a minimum to keep the business operational, but what has to be done in general to ensure the relationship continues to stay focused on achieving results.

Managing with a WIIFWe mindset focuses on managing the relationship, not the service provider. This is a critical distinction. Relationships demand involvement from the parties. Regardless of the type of relationship, one partner cannot sit in judgment of the other while absolving itself of responsibility and accountability.

Focusing on the relationship as a whole, and specifically on relationship continuity, provides several benefits. First, developing a governance structure, as described below, provides tremendous stability. Stability helps to immunize the relationship against the inevitable tensions and challenges that all relationships face over time. A focus on relationship continuity ensures that the partnership core remains resilient despite fluctuations in external and internal circumstances.

Second, the relationship is more agile. There is one speed these days: *fast!* Relationships that are slow to respond will lose their competitive advantage. Those that can react quickly to changes stay competitive. In a We relationship, the focus changes from rehashing last quarter's problems to creating mechanisms that help the partnerships respond quickly when and where necessary. Governance structures provide such a mechanism. Governance teams develop the capacity to devise quick, creative solutions to unexpected problems. More important, a governance mechanism builds trust among those who were not part of the decision-making process but have to implement the decision.

Finally, the relationship is more flexible. Realizing the need to act quickly is not enough if there is no framework to adapt the relationship to meet the challenge. It is equally important that the partnership adapt to changing environments. A focus on relationship continuity fosters sufficient adaptability and decision-making authority so the partnership can continually not only meet challenges, but also engage people and ideas. Engaging people and ideas creates a relationship that generates new ideas and ways of doing things. That generative energy is contagious, attracting the best and brightest people to the team to try to accomplish even bigger goals. As an executive related, "People came out of the woodwork wanting to join the team."

Take a moment to consider actions the relationship needs to take to ensure that all stakeholders live according to the guiding principles and maintain the integrity of the relationship.

## Topics for Discussion

- Looking ahead to the transition from negotiating the agreement to living the agreement, who are the people who might be involved in the relationship but are not now aware of our commitment to the guiding principles? Often, people who perform the daily operations are involved in the relationship, but are not necessarily on the team that agreed to the principles.
- How will we present the relationship and our commitment to the guiding principles, especially integrity in decision making?

- When should we let these people know about the collaborative nature of this partnership?
- How will we hold people accountable in our own organizations to follow the principles?
- What should we do if we have one we relationship in a sea of transaction-based relationships?

People will transition in and out of the partnership. Relationships that fail to manage personnel transitions begin to see a slackening in progress toward the goals and a weakened commitment to the principles. Below is a great example of a good relationship gone bad when a new person entered an existing relationship in a leadership position. What went wrong was not because he was new, but because he chose to do things *his way* instead of following long-standing yet informal and undocumented guiding principles and protocols.

### They Got to Yes, But...

A midsized city—like most cities—negotiated long-term agreements with its unionized firefighters. For as long as anyone could remember, the union and the city had negotiated using the principled negotiation methods outlined in *Getting to Yes*. For nearly thirty years, the city and union negotiated contracts in three-year increments. There were rarely any problems, and the negotiations followed a predictable path. Not once in all those years did the parties turn to mediation or arbitration to reach an agreement.[4]

One year the city council appointed a new city manager. He was the proverbial "new sheriff in town." Just like new sheriffs in the movies, the city manager marched in full of swagger and tough talk. The new city manager decided that the negotiations between the city and the union would be different this time around. No longer would the city and the union use the same interest-based negotiation style or the same standards for calculating cost-of-living increases, nor would the city's bargaining team have any authority to make an agreement. The city manager threw out thirty years of history, trust, and goodwill simply to prove a point: he was in charge. Getting to yes is not enough if the parties don't have some way to encourage everyone to live according to the principles, especially the principle of integrity.

After many fruitless bargaining sessions, the city's negotiation team finally agreed to have the city manager present so all participants could finally agree on some significant points. At this meeting the city manager noted the union's willingness to take furlough days to ease a tight city budget as a result of the recession. Nevertheless, the city manager took a tough stance and wanted even more concessions from the union.

The city's bargaining team was very polite and listened carefully to the union during all the negotiation sessions and then returned to the bargaining table with an equally polite no. The final round of negotiations failed to reach an agreement, and more than a year after the contract had expired, the union and the city found themselves awaiting an arbitration ruling. Morale was low to say the least. Other unions in the city geared up for their next contract negotiations assuming that the city manager would treat them the same way as the firefighters; they were ready for a fight.

What went wrong? In previous contract negotiations they eventually got to yes, but they failed to embrace a true WIIFWe mindset. A significant mistake people make is to simply follow a process of getting to yes. Without an agreement on the guiding principles that will keep the relationship on the right track when business happens—such as a city that is facing budget constraints during a recession—one party may opt to pursue a short-term solution that sacrifices the stability in the relationship. Another common mistake the city and the union made was not documenting the rules of negotiations. When the new sheriff arrived there was nothing to tell him that he was not following the rules. In the absence of such rules, the city manager felt comfortable making up new rules. The problem was that the rules were his rules, not the union's rules and not the rules that had become the cultural norm over the past thirty years.

Because of the city manager's muscular negotiation style, more than two years after the firefighter's contract expired (and as of the publication of this book), the union and the city still awaited an arbitrator's ruling. Thirty year's worth of good-will evaporated and every small issue is now a conflict. Other unions serving that same city are also involved in their own contentious contract renegotiation sessions.

In all, the transaction costs ran into the thousands of hours and tens of thousands of dollars to settle all of the issues, address formal grievances, prepare for and attend mediation and arbitration sessions.

In the final analysis an agreement is managed by people. The city's relationship with the union became contentious when the new city manager came on board. For this reason, a governance framework should contain a process for ensuring relationship continuity when changes occur inside and ousidet of the relationship. Here are the six best practices for maintaining relationship continuity when people change:

### Maintaining Relationship Continuity When People Change

- Jointly identify a limited number of personnel who are designated as key personnel for both parties.
- Establish a provision that prevents either party from unilaterally removing, replacing, or reassigning key personnel for a specific time frame. In large, complex deals this can be two to three years after the contract is signed.
- Develop a process for communicating key personnel changes. For example, establish communication protocols when key personnel become unavailable (e.g., sickness, jury duty, resignation, etc.).
- Establish a provision for replacement of key personnel. This might include having the parties provide a specific process and time frame that guides how the parties replace key people. For example, an outsource service provider may be required to provide three months' notice prior to promoting the account executive to a different account. Or the agreement may allow a client to interview a limited number of potential replacements and approve the new person.
- Establish a formal process to address personality differences between peer-to-peer pairings. The agreement should have provisions that address escalating improper behavior between the parties or between employees. Common sense says it should be intolerable for one party to allow anyone from its organization

to humiliate, denigrate, or verbally abuse team members from their partner's organization. But what about when the two "two-in-the-box" team members simply have significant style differences? In such cases if the style differences are causing a rift, it may make sense for one (or both) of the organizations to replace the individual(s) with different people who can work together more effectively.

- Organizations that embrace a WIIFWe mindset commit to live the principles in all their interactions, not just when it is convenient. Resorting to hardball tactics (such as sending in negotiators who are powerless to reach an agreement) will only make the relationship weaker when the partners go back to the day-to-day business of the relationship. The guiding principles must be at the forefront to guide all sorts of interactions ranging from renegotiating the entire contract to reevaluating metrics that are not aligned with the shared vision and may be causing "measurement minutiae."[5] When negotiators focus on the quality of the daily interactions and sound behaviors that follow the six essential guiding principles outlined in chapter 5, they are designing a relationship for continuity.

## Systems Thinking

Organizations should approach their relationship from a systems perspective. Today's complex business arrangements act more like a small ecosystem that naturally impacts other ecosystems, whether internal or external to the relationship. For example, a facilities management company provides services to many departments within a large American financial institution, and it manages other sub-contractors working on discrete projects relating to maintaining the bank's real estate portfolio.

A system is an interconnected set of elements, sub-elements and components that are coherently structured in a way that achieves a defined purpose. The interconnectivity between the elements forms a feedback loop in which information is derived. The purpose or function of the system is to perpetuate or replicate a chosen result.

Donella Meadows, the pioneering environmental scientist, author, teacher, and farmer, was an influential writer on systems thinking. Building on her initial work in 1972, Meadows' second book, *Thinking in Systems*[6] which was published posthumously in 2009, is a simple guide to help business leaders address complexity though systems thinking. Meadows illustrated her philosophy by considering the "slinky" toy. The toy appears to magically walk downstairs by itself. All that is needed is to take it out of the box, put it in the right place, and let it go with a gentle push. That gentle push releases the energy that is latent within the toy's structure to keep it moving. That latent behavior makes it possible for the slinky to "walk" down stairs by itself. It's quite simple.

A well-designed system with the right motivation has the structural ability to manage itself. Relationships *can* unlock their latent powers *when intentionally structured to do so*. But they *must be designed* properly, just like the slinky developer designed it to have latent powers to operate on its own. The slinky goes down the stairs without falling, stopping, getting tangled, or worse, falling off the stairs altogether.

So what does a slinky have to do with a business relationship? A properly designed governance structure will operate almost on its own. Face it—no business relationship operates automatically or in a vacuum. Business relationships in essence form their own systems and therefore need mechanisms in place to keep their unique system running at peak performance. In the context of the Getting to We process, systems thinking is the decision-making philosophy and mechanism for assessing the achievement of the shared vision.

What happens when the well-designed system hits a roadblock? Looking back at the slinky toy, it can move by itself so long as the stairs are straight. A bend in the stairs poses a problem for the slinky. A child has to redirect the toy to keep it moving in the right direction. Similarly, a robust relationship management redirects the relationship when "stuff happens" that could adversely impact the relationship, such as changes in the market or natural disasters.

Business relationships that embrace a WIIFWe mindset leverage systems thinking to create governance structures that allow business relationships not only to work but also to foster adaptability and agility in the face of dynamic challenges. In essence, sound relationship management practices keep the parties in the relationship—the ecosystem—in balance. They enable the partnership to be adaptive and stable at the same time. By their very nature, good relationship management structures promote systems thinking.

## RELATIONSHIP MANAGEMENT STRUCTURE

What does a good relationship management structure look like? And what are some best practice mechanisms? A sound relationship management structure creates *alignment* between the parties in a relationship, both internal and external. This often means that one or both parties may need to implement some internal restructuring to achieve alignment. Of course, the devil always lurks in the details of establishing a structure that fosters and maintains trust and integrity as the partnership evolves. Structure is not established at the snap of a finger.

The governance structure must support the parties' organizational structure as well as the shared policies and mechanisms that stress the importance of building trusting and collaborative working relationships, attitudes, and behaviors. Relationship management structures should include six components, each encompassing formal mechanisms and procedures to ensure that team members will apply the principles on the journey to reaching their goals. These are outlined in more detail below.

### Create a Tiered Management Structure

Once an initial agreement is signed, the focus changes to day-to-day operations and getting the work done. Too often the parties put the strategy on the shelf in a vinyl binder and never refer to it again until a new executive comes in and wants to create his or her own plan. This is often referred to as strategic drift. To avoid strategic drift, start by establishing an organizational structure that ensures up and down alignment between the executives and the employees in the organizations assigned to get the work done.

A tiered management structure uses a layered approach, with each tier having specific responsibilities for managing different aspects of the business. This structure creates alignment among the upper management, middle management, and day-to-day workforce. Each layer is accountable for examining the relationship and business success from its own point of view and is accountable for ensuring that the relationship is focused on the strategic and transformational components as well as the tactical elements. Using a tiered structure also greatly facilitates the timely resolution of problems. No matter how often people communicate, not all issues can be resolved at the lowest levels in the relationship. Some matters need to move to a higher level in the relationship to get resolved.

Larger, more complex relationships typically have three tiers, and smaller relationships often involve two (management and day-to-day operational level). The three most common levels include:

*Board of advisors.* The board provides overall sponsorship, strategic direction, and feedback regarding progress against the shared vision and corresponding goals, and overall performance. This group also makes decisions related to escalated issues and approves of large transformational projects. The board should meet at least quarterly for the first two years of the agreement and semiannually after that. It should consist of senior executives from the parties.

*Joint operations committee.* This committee provides direction regarding service delivery and monitors progress of the relationship and the work. It is responsible for service quality across all locations. The group also sets continuous innovation and implementation priorities. The committee should meet monthly for the first year of the project and quarterly thereafter, pending mutual agreement.

*Management groups.* These groups oversee day-to-day operations in each location. There may be several working management groups. For example, there might be regional service delivery management groups and project-based groups that identify and implement improvement and innovation initiatives.

Using a three-tiered approach ensures that each level in the organization provides guidance across three key areas—functional working levels, operational levels, and executive levels—in a timely and consistent manner.

## Establish Clear Roles

The relationship management structure should support the nature of the work and also be designed to keep the parties in sync throughout the life of the relationship. There is no "right answer" for the roles parties should have in relationship mangement; however, establishing clear roles is essential. The Microsoft OneFinance outsourcing relationship with Accenture provides guidance. The companies' global relationship spans back office finance operations across 96 subsidiaries and consists of clear roles for "managing" the work *and the relationship*.[7]

### Service Delivery Management
Three individuals from each company are responsible for the efficient and effective delivery of service, for responsive customer service, and for ensuring that service delivery complies with regulatory and internal policy requirements.

### Transformation Management
Three people are responsibile for identifying and sponsoring ideas, innovations, and process changes across both Microsoft and Accenture. One person from each company is devoted to each of the three main process areas under the scope of the relationship (accounts payable, accounts receivable, and the buy center). The goal of this function is to identify and deploy transformation projects that will help Microsoft and Accenture work together to achieve their shared vision and transformation goals.

### Commercial and Compliance Management
One person from each company is dedicated to managing the commercial and contractual aspects of the relationship. In the OneFinance relationship, the commercial managers at Mirosoft and Accenture with this role are assigned to monitor the scope of the work and pricing changes, and ensure that the agreement stays up-to-date as business needs change.

### Relationship Management
Each company will typically assign a relationship manager who formally manages the overall relationship dynamic and ensures that the parties follow the guiding principles. This role is often combined with the commercial and compliance manager in less complex relationships.

Regardless of the roles chosen to manage the business and relationship, they should be embedded in each "layer" of the organization. The larger the deal, the more people in each of the roles. For example, Microsoft has eight full-time people as part of its governance team (with Accenture having personel mirroring the same roles in a peer-to-peer arrangement). Often the first reaction is, "Gosh, we can't put that kind of overhead on our project!" Managing the work and the relationship itself is not free; it's essential to devote the right resources not only to getting the work done, but also to managing the relationship. While the Microsoft OneFinance relationship is large in scale, how the companies structured their roles is instructive.

## Establish Peer-to-Peer Communication Protocols

Once the tiered structure is established along with the various functional roles within it, the parties should focus on horizontal integration. One way to do this is to map the various individuals using a peer-to-peer communication alignment approach. A peer-to-peer communication model (often referred to as a "two-in-a-box" or "reverse bow-tie" approach) improves the flow of information and empowers the parties to streamline communications and remain "aligned" over time. Basically, one peer from one partner is paired with one peer from the other partner, forming the "two-in-a-box structure." For example, people with daily supervisory responsibilities are paired together, while people with more global supervisory responsibility and accountability are paired and so on.

This two-in-a-box structure has several functions. At the lowest levels of responsibility and accountability, the pair functions as a business management and problem-solving unit. The goal is to ensure that problems are first resolved at the lowest possible level of authority. Enforcing a peer-to-peer structure improves accountability and enables the pair to work together more cohesively.

At higher levels, the pair monitors performance against larger goals. At the highest level, the two-in-a-box pair functions as a strategic leadership team keeping the relationship's vision aligned to other strategic initiatives companies may undertake. This structure allows more senior levels of the governance team to focus on strategy, planning, and transformation initiatives rather than on micromanaging daily business operations.

Peer-to-peer pairing allows the relationship to be more agile and adaptive, while simultaneously reducing conflict requiring senior management's intervention. However, in order for this structure to work, each partner must be willing to empower the peer-to-peer relationship relative to its level of responsibility and accountability. Peer-to-peer mapping must be performed for *each* level established for the relationship.

Often companies establish peer-to-peer communication protocols only at operational levels, focusing on performance management and resolving day-to-day tactical issues. Although most of the communication will occur at the operational level, the real benefit of using a peer-to-peer approach is that it streamlines communication across *all* layers. At the lower levels, the conversations tend to be about day-to-day tasks, while the higher levels channel discussions around providing executive direction. The executive level is critical to helping achieve the shared vision.

In relationships with multiple parties and/or with many stakeholders, organizations often also use an advisory board to communicate problems and make decisions. Depending on the circumstances, the advisory board can have a two-in-a-box pairing, in addition to inviting other stakeholders to join the board. A good example of this in action is Water for People, which commonly establishes Community Water Boards for its partnerships with local communities.[8]

Water For People establishes these self-governing community water boards in order to hold all the stakeholders accountable. In community development work, the community can be lulled into thinking that someone else should solve its problems. The nonprofit learned that the solution is much more effective when stakeholders have skin in the game, so to speak.

Because Water For People partners with governments and communities to bring sustainable drinking water and waste water sanitation to poor rural areas, the community water board works as an independent advisory body. The community water board sets appropriate household fees (tariffs) to cover the costs of water system maintenance and repair. Each board has authority to decide the amount each user must pay and when that tariff is collected in order to have adequate spare parts available. For example, if a household is headed by a child, the board may subsidize or waive the water fees. This advisory council is self-governing. And because it is established by the community to serve the community its decisions are trusted and respected.

## Develop a Communication Cadence, Tempo, or Rhythm

As with any team, regularly scheduled conference calls, team meetings, and face-to-face formal reviews are grease for the wheels. Successful

Figure 9.1  Global relationship management

**Executive Steering Committee**

| MRK Contact | Supplier Contact | Purpose | | Twice a year |
|---|---|---|---|---|
| CEO/CFO/CIO<br>Sr. VP GP[1]<br>Director Stakeholder[2]<br>Director GP<br>Relationship Manager[3] | CEO/Owner<br>VP Sales & Marketing | Purpose<br>• Executive sponsorship<br>• Establish partnership vision and goals<br>• Generate collaboration options<br>• Address collaboration obstacles<br>  – Resolve organizational issues<br>  – Provide resources<br>• Approval of collaboration programs<br>• Address major performance issues | • Meeting notes<br>• Partnership goals<br>• Action plans<br>• Opportunity lists | Twice a year |

**Operation Committee**

| MRK Contact | Supplier Contact | Purpose | | Quarterly |
|---|---|---|---|---|
| Director Stakeholder[1]<br>Director GP | VP Sales & Marketing | Purpose<br>• Set direction and priorities; drive compliance | • Meeting notes<br>• Opportunity assessments<br>• Collaboration plans | Quarterly |

| Members | Members | Activities | Outputs | Frequency |
|---|---|---|---|---|
| Relationship Mgr[2]<br>Sourcing Mgr[3] | Account Managers | – Identify/assess collaboration opportunities<br>– Develop collaboration programs<br>• Execute collaboration programs<br>– Assign/deploy resources<br>– Conduct performance reviews<br>• Conduct performance reviews; address issues<br>• Drive development of annual plan | • Justifications<br>• Action plan<br>• STPs<br>• Performance reviews | |
| **Sourcing/Functional Teams** | | | | |
| MRK Contact<br>Relationship Mgr[1,2]<br>Sourcing Mgr<br>Key Stakeholders[3]<br>Technical experts | Supplier Contact<br>Account Managers<br>Technical Managers<br>Technical experts | Purpose<br>• Prepare performance reviews<br>– Address performance reviews<br>– Lead collaboration programs<br>– Manage win/win relationship | • Meeting notes<br>• Scoreboard and agenda<br>• Performance development plan<br>• Action plans | Monthly or as often as needed |

Notes:
[1] Driver
[2] Facilitator
[3] Secretary

Source: "3PL Collaboration Scoring Model." Arlington VA: The Corporate Executive Board.

relationships need free-flowing communication between operational groups, their managers, and the executives of the companies. The most successful relationships have formal mechanisms (and informal protocols) for talking daily, weekly, monthly, quarterly, and annually.

All relationships, regardless of size, should establish a regular communication cadence process that becomes the heartbeat of how the parties communicate. We like to think of the communication cadence as the rhythm of the business because it helps the parties establish a formal mechanism for managing the business. The frequency of meetings should vary based on the nature, size, and complexity of the relationship. At a minimum, the executive layer should meet quarterly, the operating committee should meet monthly, and the functional teams should meet weekly and even daily if needed. For example, Merck—a large pharmaceutical company—established a formalized cadence for working with its strategic suppliers, as shown in figure 9.1.

The Merck example shows the need to formalize the timing and nature of communication with partners in order to make these interactions both regular and effective. Continuous interaction between Merck and its suppliers makes it much easier for the company to identify collaboration opportunities and generate operational efficiencies. As an added benefit, Merck's close relationships with its suppliers puts it in a position to foster collaboration among several suppliers, thus enabling providers to find joint opportunities to reduce waste and inefficiencies in the Merck supply chain.

## Establish a Transparent Performance Management Program to Foster Feedback

Collecting and using data to provide feedback on the overall performance (both in terms of the output of the relationship as well as the overall relationship itself) often leads to a realization that each business is not thinking in terms of entire processes or systems. In other words, many organizations are locked into thinking in terms of functions or jobs. Businesses are structured for people to perform a function or a job without ever thinking about how that function or job relates to all the other functions and jobs within a process or system.

Beginning to change from that small field of vision to a larger one yields transformational results. One supply chain executive said off-handedly, "It took us some time, but once we started thinking in terms of the whole process and then how that process fit into the system, we started to see some real results. People knew how they fit into the whole process and did what was needed."[9]

Highly collaborative relationships require a structure that generates regular feedback for the benefit of the enterprise. Feedback must be accurate—based on commonly accepted data points—and it must be shared with people who are responsible for achieving the goals. Unfortunately, businesses often have some feedback structure in place, but don't use it. One executive sheepishly admitted that he could not remember the last time that his team and the customer's team had a governance meeting.

Chapter 3 explored the virtues of transparency for building trust in a relationship. Transparency moves to the forefront in jointly creating business plans and managing the reporting crucial to operate the business and the relationship. Organizations should pay special attention to issues of information accuracy and appropriate feedback. Accuracy means using data that everyone can rely and agree upon. Gathering data that everyone agrees upon is much more difficult than most people anticipate. In a commercial relationship, the customer is often struggling to collect data. Conflicting reporting standards can create internal havoc and diminish trust between the partners.

A senior purchasing executive for a computer software company noted, "My number one challenge was collecting data [to share with our partner]. We had data all over the place. We tended to collect data by function and not by process." It took him more than six months just to track down the sources of much of the data! Then there were the issues of reliability. The executive continued, "Because we collected by function, the data was not the same. Some functions had different reasons for collecting the same numbers so the numbers would appear a little different. It caused us some problems at first, but we worked it out in the end."[10]

If communication greases the wheel of collaboration, then the unilateral collection and use of data is sand, clogging the axle and slowing the rotation. Accuracy as an element of honesty requires people to accept some common observable facts. If data collection is not entirely visible to one partner and if some of the data can be interpreted differently, there is little likelihood that data will become a common observable fact.

Therefore, to keep the relationship focused on its goals, partners share the responsibility of collecting and analyzing data. Shared data means the companies create one set of data to analyze for trends, performance issues, and market opportunities. Markets change, end users' demands change, commodities become more or less scarce. The partners have an equal responsibility and opportunity in reporting one set of data for the relationship. This is not a duplication of efforts. It is working jointly with agreed-upon data.

Not all data should be collected, especially as part of a joint effort. The focus should be on collecting data that is important to assess the partnership's progress toward meeting goals and realizing the shared vision. If the relationship has a goal of improving customer satisfaction, then collecting only one set of data regarding customer satisfaction scores would be appropriate.

## DEVELOP A PRINCIPLED APPROACH TO MANAGING CONFLICTS

Conflict is inevitable. Conflict rarely occurs when things are going smoothly. But it's a different story when something is missing, is late, is broken, off target, or when one partner diverts time, effort, and money to another opportunity.

The difference between a transactional approach to conflict and a relationship approach is stark. In a transaction-based relationship conflict is avoided in the hopes that it will simply go away on its own or until it's time to change partners. When that tactic doesn't work, or when the conflict turns into a crisis, conflict is quickly escalated—potentially involving legal action. That is never a positive sign. But this is not the same as being agile and adaptive; quite the contrary.

In a highly collaborative relationship, people understand from the outset that "stuff" happens. Even in the highest functioning relationships problems can arise that require more formal attention. Those organizations take a different approach to conflict. They design a process to address the unpredictable, the unexpected, and any conflicts. When the relationship is initially formed, the relationship structure includes a proactive process for problem solving and dispute resolution.

Once again, the guiding principles play a significant role. Solving problems will ultimately rest upon the qualities of trust, loyalty, and integrity. Companies that trust one another will also trust the process. Trusting the process is a sign of loyalty to the relationship and its goals. Finally, integrity will trigger predictable decisions and actions.

A good process for solving problems and disputes outlines a clear decision-making procedure and timeline. Devising this process now—when there is no dispute—creates a sense of joint accountability. This process empowers the peer-to-peer pair to solve problems at the earliest stages and includes an agreed upon escalation procedure when the problem requires attention from senior leadership.

Successful relationships map out the process for resolving a conflict. For example, if the middle management two-in-a-box pair cannot resolve the problem for any reason, then the senior management two-in-a-box pair must resolve the problem. However, a good governance process, coupled with adherence to the guiding principles, will often prevent a problem from developing into a conflict demanding senior level attention. Nevertheless, putting an escalation process in writing actually forces middle management to stay in a conversation until the problem is resolved. High impact, urgent problems will require a more immediate response. Therefore, a timeline that does not allow problems to languish is essential.

Figure 9.2 shows the escalation process. Each set of boxes is a two-in-a-box pair. That pair is given a time frame within which to solve the problem. If they cannot solve the issue, the problem is then sent up to the next level for resolution. Most of the time, problems are resolved at the appropriate two-in-a-box pair. This relieves senior leadership from having to resolve problems that involve daily operational issues.

This approach prevents parties from ignoring problems until they reach the point of requiring an intervention. Because the partners have established the process in the beginning, they often are far more likely to follow it. More important, an active problem-solving mindset prevents people from falling into bad habits and WIIFMe thinking.

Finally, companies should consider when to involve a neutral third party, such as professional mediators or facilitators. A mediator or

Figure 9.2   Escalation process

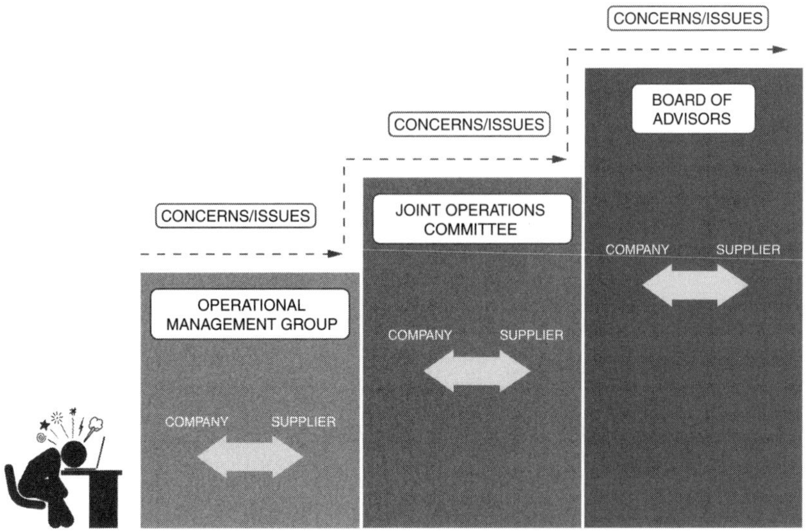

facilitator is not a judge or arbitrator. Judges and arbitrators issue rulings. Rather, neutral third parties facilitate conversations that encourage the partners to leverage the strength of the relationship while applying the guiding principles to the problem. They help the parties stay true to their intentions and guide them to a solution.

Since many business relationships limit their conflict resolution process to a clause or two in a contract, discussing these topics will prove useful. The goal of any conflict resolution process is to solve as many problems at the lowest level of responsibility and accountability as possible. The result is to free the more senior levels of responsibility and accountability to make strategic decisions rather than fight fires.

The box below suggests some topics for discussion when developing a relationship management framework.

**Topics for Relationship Management Discussion**

- What parts of an effective relationship management mechanism do we (the relationship) have now?
- What parts are missing? And what do we want to focus on developing first?

- What tiered management structure will work best for the relationship?
- How will that management structure be organized?
- How will we (the partnership) define the roles associated with the tiered management structure? (Use titles not necessarily names as people change in and out of roles.)
- How will we organize the relationship to work in some form of a peer-to-peer relationship?
- What will each party have to do to organize itself internally to be effective in a peer-to-peer relationship?
- What do we feel is necessary for effective communication?
- How will we provide each other feedback using shared data?
- How do we want to structure an effective proactive process for problem solving?

The answers will help the relationship develop a strong and flexible relationship management structure.

## THE END AND THE BEGINNING

The Getting to We process is complete. Embracing the WIIFWe mindset will soon reap the rewards that collaborative business relationships deserve. It is the end of a process, but not the end of the journey. The journey to achieve a shared vision has only begun. The two case studies profiled in chapter 10 demonstrate how companies have worked together to *embrace and live* the WIIFWe mindset—and have achieved tremendous success.

# CHAPTER 10

# THE POWER OF WE

With a WIIFWe mindset and the Getting to We process in place, the companies profiled in this chapter have developed highly collaborative and sustainable business relationships. By embracing the WIIFWe philosophy, they formed a framework for collaborative and trusting relationships.

And by focusing on negotiating their *relationships*, these companies recognized new opportunities to expand and improve their businesses and obtained high levels of efficiency and problem solving. It all started with a what's-in-it for-we mindset.

A large US telecom company (TeleCo) and its facilities management service provider (FM Provider) were in an existing relationship when TeleCo's new president of real estate and facilities (we'll call him Steve) joined the team. He saw the potential that the WIIFWe mindset could bring to TeleCo's relationship with FM Provider. His foresight, together with a team dedicated to operational excellence, reinvented their relationship.

## TELECO AND FACILITES MANAGEMENT PROVIDER

The relationship between these companies provide an excellent example of the Getting to We process.[1] In 2010, TeleCo was assessing several of its outsourcing relationships. One of those was with FM Provider, its facilities and real estate management service provider. As part of the review process, the companies agreed to use a Certified Deal Architect (CDA) as a netural third party to conduct a review of its relationship. The deal review included a review of the contract, the formal governance structure, and the informal cultural norms for working together. The companies also participated in a Compatibility and Trust Assessment™ (CaT).

They knew there were problems, but did not know what to do about them. The FM Provider's director of operational excellence (we'll call her Jenny) took part in the deal review and after seeing the results observed, "It was shocking to see just how strained our relationship was." The teams recognized the need to rebuild trust and change the partnership's culture. Executive leadership from the companies decided to champion a WIIFWe mindset. Jenny said, "The senior leadership team gave the entire team permission to change." The FM Provider's account director for the TeleCo relationship, (we'll call him Rod) said, "The failure in other organizations is that they just make a pronouncement and think it's done. It's not a snap your fingers and make it happen event. Things have to change. Management has to set the tone. Management has to communicate effectively with a clear message that is reinforced."

Steve brought Jenny into the conversation to change the relationship's culture because of her background in operational excellence. Steve then paired his colleague and the TeleCo's director of business intelligence, process, and strategy, (we'll call her Diane) with Jenny. Jenny and Diane quickly realized that changing the partnership's culture would take thoughtful effort.

Diane noted, "We [Diane and Jenny] understood what it took to initiate cultural change and understood what it would take to make it happen." They began to champion and model WIIFWe behaviors in a conscious effort to change the cultural norms of the relationship. Diane continued, "Coming from the perspective of operational excellence, we [Diane and Jenny] can have a more objective perspective when working with the teams."

Diane and Jenny worked to drive a significant level of change throughout the TeleCo's relationship with the FM Provider over the course of two years. "It's fantastic to have the intent to collaborate," Diane later said. "But you have to have the language and tools to live that intention." Jenny and Diane agreed to model the behavior that senior leadership expected from the entire team on a daily basis. They held themselves accountable for demonstrating the right behaviors and seek out opportunities to call out behaviors based on the cultural norms they were trying to establish.

Rod liked what he saw. "Senior leadership walked the talk. We all took opportunities for coaching seriously. Every week we'd see people acting in an old noncollaborative manner, and we coached them to behave in a new manner."

But it became apparent that modeling behavior was not enough. Not everyone on the team had bought into a WIIFWe mindset; there were some people who had a hard time letting go of old behaviors. In 2011, the companies brought most of the team together for a collaborative communications workshop facilitated by a CDA. The purpose of the workshop was to give the larger team specific collaborative communication tools.

The CDA recommended the partners bring a "real" issue the parties were working through. The sheer number of metrics that the FM Provider tracked was causing tensions between people at both companies. There were many disagreements about the significance of tracking specific metrics. The parties had fallen into what is commonly known as measurement minutiae,[2] with more than 400 detailed and contractually binding Service Level Agreements (SLAs).

The companies had to address the SLAs using a different set of rules. The workshop gave them tangible negotiation and communication strategies and tactics. It reinforced Diane and Jenny's beliefs that many of the conventional negotiation strategies they employed were causing additional friction in the relationship.

After the workshop Jenny observed, "The atmosphere changed. People had permission to talk about the hard things and authentically share what is and is not working."

At a second all-hands meeting a year later, Jenny and Diane wanted to demonstrate the negotiation rule of sitting side by side rather than across the table from each other. They did this with a rope. Attached to the middle of the rope was a magenta box inscribed with two high-level goals or desired outcomes.

Diane and Jenny faced each other while discussing some issues facing the partnership. Each woman was pulling on the rope. Diane reported, "The desired outcomes don't move much but it feels like we were making progress because there was effort." Then Jenny put her side of the rope down walked over to Diane and picked up the rope with Diane. Jenny said, "Then we pulled together on the magenta box with the desired outcomes written down on it and the box went somewhere!" The audience got the message. She continued, "Now, the box lives on the floor [the combined team is now located at the TeleCo's headquarters] and is a fixture at meetings."

"We are together," Jenny said. "There is no posturing; there's just no need for it. Everyone has permission to question—analytically question—why we are doing something. If the activity or project does not meet the desired outcomes, then it is not pursued. There is no energy spent on fighting for the activity or the project."

Diane agreed: "We've done the cultural and change management aspect well…We are practicing the techniques. Metaphorically, we are moving from the bunny ski slope to the adult ski slope, but we are not at the black diamond technically difficult hill yet. We keep encouraging people to act more collaboratively because it is easier for some people to go back to the old customer/vendor relationship. But in that relationship we don't get transformational results."

These two companies also found that conflict was greatly reduced as a result of the change management initiative. Rod noted, "It is an amazing thing to go from a governance organization of escalation protocols if we don't agree (which is an unfortunate by-product of dysfunction) to a virtual governance process where people are able to resolve the issue at the right time with the right person in the right two-in-a-box matrix. We've eliminated the 'me' attitudes."

He added, "The most important aspect starts with the mindset. To be successful, both partners have to believe that a collaborative partnership is the right thing to do. It's a choice. And it is important to recognize that it will take some work to get there."

By taking the change management aspect of the relationship seriously and encouraging collaborative behaviors, TeleCo and FM Provider began living the WIIFWe mindset. Working relationships improved and productivity soared. The members of the leadership team are proud as they look at how far they've some. People are working as one team to achieve the partnership's goals. This is truly and powerfully what living as We is all about. Their relationship is designed to function by itself at all levels to achieve a predictable set of results.

## THE RELIANCECM JOURNEY

Getting to We is not just for large companies. Small and midsized companies have also benefitted from the WIIFWe mindset. RelianceCM (RCM) is a small manufacturing company that applied the WIIFWe mindset to improve existing relationships and new customer acquisition.[3]

Several years ago Scott Schroeder, president of contract manufacturing at RCM, couldn't believe what he was reading. Here was a book describing the very philosophy that he himself embraced. That book, *Vested Outsourcing: Five Rules That Will Transform Outsourcing*,[4] spoke to him at a deep level, yet his company was not even in the outsourcing business. His company was at the other end of the contracting spectrum—it did small prototype projects for other companies. He wondered how he could leverage the Vested mindset, methodology, and business model to meet RCM's needs and the needs of his customers. Ultimately, Schroeder decided that the best fit for his company was to select a couple of customers and get to We.

RCM's journey to understand and apply the WIIFWe mindset and the process to get to We resembles most such journeys. From the beginning, Schroeder recognized that the WIIFWe mindset matched his personal philosophy. It was not as if the WIIFWe mindset was new; it wasn't. What was new was that a book was so open about explaining and advocating the mindset. Not many of his company's customers embraced it. Schroeder noted, "Some customers don't care about service and quality. They want their services as cheap as they can get it, and some could not care less if their suppliers went bankrupt in the process—they would just find another supplier."

The first step Schroeder took was to recognize that he could leverage the WIIFWe mindset into opportunities to work with a few select customers in a different way than his company had in the past. But that realization led Schroeder to ask an important question, "Who would want to work with us this way?" Finding the right kind of customer and the right kind of opportunity for both RCM and its customers was paramount.

It took time for Schroeder to find the right kind of current and new customers to negotiate We relationships. Schroeder described one of the first tests for selecting a customer for a WIIFWe relationship, quipping, "We take them out to dinner. And if they are not someone we would take home to our family, we are not going to have a collaborative relationship with them."

Schroeder looks for the right fit. Does the customer align with Schroeder's mindset? If customers don't, they may still be a good fit for contract manufacturing in general, just not for a We partnership. For customers not comfortable with the WIIFWe mindset or unwilling to embrace the mindset, he wryly notes, "We still work with them. It is give and take. We still give, and they still take."

Once he identifies a customer that is likely a good fit for a We partnership, and there is an appropriate opportunity for long-term mutual benefits, Schroeder decides to test the water. In other words, he will choose to share something with the customer that he would not normally share. Then the customer's reaction is closely watched. If the customer reacts badly—judges the shared information harshly or appears offended, for example, Schroeder takes a step back to reassess. "It depends," he explains. "Some people are just reserved and it takes time to trust. It might take one or two more tries before I get a good feel for them. If they become more open and receptive, then so am I." If the customer reacts positively to the shared information, Schroeder will share more information and his business philosophy of mutual gain.

This is a critical step in the process. It is impossible to have a one-sided collaborative relationship. The companies have to agree on the underlying WIIFWe mindset and a shared vision for the relationship. It doesn't have to take endless discussions over weeks and months to get to an agreement on the shared vision and the guiding principles that will form the foundation for the relationship. It can happen quickly, and typically for Schroeder it happens over the course of several conversations.

Once he feels comfortable that the customer also believes in the WIIFWe mindset and the opportunity is ripe for mutual gain, Schroeder "opens the company's kimono," so to speak. Referring to a particular highly collaborative relationship with a customer, Schroeder said, "We both agreed to be completely transparent. We shared target costs and needs, issues within each company. It's like having a dialogue with your best friend. There is no defensiveness when discussing really difficult questions. We share data and the methodology behind the numbers. We openly question assumptions." This level of transparency and openness has built tremendous levels of trust between RCM and its customer.

From there RCM and the customer negotiate a master services agreement (MSA), which serves as a flexible framework for the relationship. The remaining transactions, in the form of purchase orders and invoices, flow between them, and the MSA is the governing agreement.

This particular arrangement makes it easier to be flexible and adaptable while still providing mutual benefits.

Schroeder has an interesting take on how his company approaches discussing money—typically the most contentious parts of the negotiations—with customers who share the WIIFWe mindset. He does not believe the conversations about money he has had with We customers are even negotiations. "We shared all the numbers like our markup on labor, etc. The customer said ok—no questions asked. Their thought is that it is ok for us to make a margin—not obscene margins—as long as we are still hitting their pricing targets." Schroeder and his team work to build a total package for the customer. He likes the flexibility of looking at the total costs to build the price. "Some customers love this approach. Those that do are thinking in terms of mutual benefit."

A big part of RCM's success is Schroeder's integrity when working with RCM's suppliers. Schroeder buys parts that go into the customer's prototypes. He could easily justify using a muscular negotiation style to extract significant cost savings from RCM's suppliers and have RCM pocket the difference between what RCM pays the supplier and what RCM charges its customer for the part. When buying parts, he says, "When it comes down to price, we rarely need to drive a price down to save some money. The very first thing we do if we see a price that we think is high is double-check the scope of work we sent over to them [the supplier]. Then I ask them 'Help us understand how you got to this price' and the supplier will explain."

This is a fundamental part of RCM's success. Schroeder and his team work together with suppliers for the benefit of the relationship with their customers. Once he understands a supplier's thinking, he looks at the total picture to reduce costs. He might change the scope of the project or eliminate an unneeded step in the process to reduce the price without taking advantage of the supplier.

Schroeder is enthusiastic about the results of his efforts to establish a WIIFWe mindset with select clients. He said, "When I first learned about Vested, I viewed a Vested agreement as the ultimate goal. But I am small business—a very small business. And a lot of elements cannot be applied to my business because contractually it would be like the tail wagging the dog with my clients, and there would be no way to get my clients' lawyers to change their standard contract templates.

"But I thought, 'I can still achieve the mindset!'" The WIIFWe mind-set is the core concept of Vested, Getting to We, and of RCM. Schroeder added, "It took work, but I did it and it has paid dividends. We literally doubled our revenue the first year from the clients we chose to work with differently. And we would not have achieved that success without the WIIFWe mindset."

The companies profiled here, and many more, made the shift to WIIFWe and they live We. By negotiating their relationships, they built sufficient understanding, comfort, and trust to work collaboratively not just in the present—but also in the future. Their collaborative efforts mean that they can continue to prosper, regardless of inevitable future changes.

Companies adopting the WIIFWe mindset discover discovered something vital: the secret to a good deal is negotiating relationships in order to deliver a sustainable competitive advantage for everyone long after the deal is signed. Getting to We. Living as We. The Power of We.

# WE ARE ALL WINNERS

We hope you believe in the power of the WIIFWe mindset. Corporations, governments, and nonprofits alike have achieved extraordinary results by forming partnerships that embody WIIFWe and follow the process of Getting to We. Ray Kroc, founder of the McDonald's restaurant chain, knew many years ago that to succeed in the game of business, sometimes businesses are not in business alone. Rather, an interconnected "System" of businesses, organizations, and employees all come together to achieve success for everyone involved.

Unfortunately, businesses too often ask themselves and each other, "Who is winning?" This pits them against their competitors, employees, and suppliers. In fact, the authors of *Getting to Yes*[1] warn negotiators not to ask who is winning as this is "inappropriate" and sets the business down the wrong path.

Rather than asking who is winning, the better question is: "How can I leverage the power of a business relationship so that everyone wins?" *Getting to We* answers that question.

## VALUE, VALUE, VALUE

*Getting to We* helps organizations embrace the WIIFWe philosophy and mindset by providing a process that will unleash tremendous economic value for the parties and their partnership and for myriad other stakeholders—from employees to citizens and shareholders. We cannot stress enough that highly collaborative relationships have both a WIIFWe mindset and a process for continuous collaboration. You cannot have one without the other.

*Getting to We* shifts the focus away from how *you* can solve *my* problem to how *we* can solve the problem. This means that companies must negotiate the relationship and let all the transactions, whether large or small, follow. *The power is in the relationship.* Like the slinky toy, once the framework is in place, the self-perpetuating system will generate good results for everyone. And a sound governance structure will ensure that businesses navigate unpredictable terrain just as children must redirect the slinky toy so it can successfully manuevuer curves and turns in the staircase. By working together businesses can learn to trust their partners not to take advantage of them when times are tough. They face challenges together to develop a competitive advantage in the market place for themselves.

Some may think Getting to We is naïve. We understand and embrace that businesses are in business to make money. And that is precisely why we are so passionate about Getting to We. We want sustainable, long-term business partnerships *because* they unlock and create long-term value where everyone else thought there was none left.

We are inspired by Water for People's commitment to 100 percent sustainable drinking water and waste water removal. We recognize the value Kaiser-Hill's 200 inventions bring to the larger business community, and we value Dell and GENCO ATC's efforts to reduce scrap and waste from refurbishing computers.

What value could you unlock if you only looked at the situation from a different perspective?

## BEYOND YES

Our intention is to channel people's genuine desire to resolve the inherent conflict between "negotiating" and the need to develop sustainable business relationships that go beyond simply getting to yes. We've heard from many business people who are frustrated when they go to the negotiation table, who realize that value in interest-based negotiating principles are stuck using tactics that try to divide that one precious orange more creatively, rather than demanding ways to invest in the partnership by planting the seeds that will bear more fruit for everyone.

By challenging conventional thinking, we've created a new "gold standard" for negotiating partnership relationships. The foundation of that gold standard begins with trust, transparency and compatability.

From there, the parties agree to and live according to the six guiding principles. These principles provide the ethical setting that people have been looking for to move beyond traditional negotiation strategies and tactics. The principles tell partners how to act and behave in relation to one another while forming the relationship and then living it. The principles are simple, fair and robust. They also reflect societal morals and therefore are worthy of following.

It's time to embrace the WIIFWe mindset. It *is* a choice and one that is not made lightly. The process of Getting to We is not always easy. Rewiring old ways of thinking and reestablishing existing ways of doing things requires time and energy. Yet, those that have embodied WIIFWe and walked the path never look back.

You now have the key to unlock extraordinary potential. Will you use it?

# ACKNOWLEDGMENTS

Writing *Getting to We* has been a truly collaborative effort. We embodied the We mindset; our conversations were rich, textured, and focused on achieving our vision of shedding light on a new approach to negotiating partnerships.

We would like to thank the many talented people whose pioneering efforts paved the way for this book. We've incorporated research from many diverse disciplines. Our deepest gratitude goes first to those who took the time to conduct the underlying research that has bloomed into no fewer than five books, including this one.

Mike Ledyard and Karl Manrodt—coauthors of the first book on Vested Outsourcing—were part of the original research and without that research this book would not be possible. Jacqui Archer—coauthor of *The Vested Outsourcing Manual*—helped set the stage for this book by sharing her real-life experiences with establishing guiding principles in many long-term strategic partnerships. And finally, thank you Katherine Kawamoto—coauthor of *The Vested Outsourcing Manual*—for your guidance and enthusiasm.

We would like to give Tim Cummins, founder and chief executive of IACCM, very special thanks for his guidance, advice, and tireless support in spreading the message about how contracting and legal professionals need to embrace the WIIFWe mindset when working with strategic partnerships. We genuinely appreciate all you've done for us personally and for the commercial contracting and management professions.

A very special thanks to all the progressive organizations that provided us with case studies, best practices, and a vision for excellence:

McDonald's and its Supplier Advisory Council
Procter & Gamble and Jones Lang LaSalle
Dell and GENCO ATC
Microsoft and Accenture and the award-winning
  OneFinance Project

Kaiser-Hill and all the people who made the Rocky Flats cleanup
   project a success
Water For People
RelianceCM

Many more people helped with this effort and must remain unnamed
due to their corporate rules and desire to maintain their competitive
advantages. You know who you are. Thank you.

We thank the University of Tennessee for its continued support of
our zealous research and outreach efforts to spread the word about the
transformational powers of the WIIFWe philosophy.

Elizabeth Kanna: You offered the vision for what could be and the
tools and guidance necessary to make that vision a reality.

Laurie Harting: You were quick to understand the power of the
Vested philosophy and provided valuable strategic direction on this
book. With Palgrave Macmillan we live WIIFWe.

Bill DiBenedetto: Thank you very much. You are more than an edi-
tor; you are a strategic advisor who embraces and respects our philosophy, which means so much to us.

Elizabeth Kanna and Jason Wister. Thanks for your fabulous design
work on the book cover.

Jeanne Kling: Thank you for your hours of diligent research and
documentation of the stories that give this book its richness and depth.

We'd also like to thank Adrianne Gross and Astrid Uka for brain-
storming with us, strategically editing the book and all of their insights
that made the book so much better.

Lastly, we would like to thank the people who have supported us for
many years:

Carol Bowser and Mikelann Valtera for seeing the power of these
concepts and encouraging Jeanette to share them. Liz Gutheridge,
Cheryl Binda, and Pam Pacquett for countless hours of brainstorm-
ing and support on Jeanette's journey. And Jill Konrath, who "forced"
Jeanette to write her first book, starting her on the path to authorship.

Mike Watts, Rhonda Watts, and Liz Roteman for keeping Kate on
time and in the right place.

Thank you to the Swedish law firm Advokatfirman Lindahl KB for
supporting all of David's efforts.

And last, but certainly not least, a special thanks to our families for all your support and patience during this fabulous experience:

Tim, Isabella, and Elizabeth Lohraff
Greg and Austin Picinich
Caroline, Rebecka, Oskar, and Klara Frydlinger

# NOTES

## 1  WHAT ARE YOU G-E-T-T-I-N-G TO?

1. "Supply Chain Council Announces 2011 North American Supply Chain Excellence Award Winners." *Supply Chain Council*, May 26, 2011, press release. Available at http://supply-chain.org/awards/2011-na-winners.
2. Research interview.
3. Adam Smith's *An Inquiry into the Nature of the Wealth of Nations* (1776) is in the public domain and widely available online, such as at http://bartleby.com/10/101.html.
4. The game gets its name because two players are each charged with committing a crime. When questioned by the police, each has the chance to confess his own involvement, implicate his partner in crime and receive a reduced sentence, or remain silent. The Prisoner's Dilemma scenario is a classic exercise in game theory that illustrates the advantages and disadvantages of cooperation. It helps individuals and businesses understand what governs the balance between cooperation and competition in business, in politics, and in social settings. The game demonstrates how two individuals might not cooperate even if it appears that it is in their best interests to do so. It was originally framed by Merrill Flood and Melvin Dresher working at RAND in 1950. Albert W. Tucker formalized the game with prison sentence payoffs and gave it the name Prisoner's Dilemma.
5. Cooperation would mean remaining silent about one's own involvement and the involvement of the other player in the crime.
6. Robert Axelrod, *The Evolution of Cooperation* (New York: Basic Books, 1984).
7. Ibid, 119.
8. Reseach interview with confidential source.
9. See Vested case studies and white papers on collaboration, including "Vested For Success: McDonald's Secret Sauce for Supply Chain Success" and "Unpacking Oliver: Ten Lessons to Improve Collaborative Outsourcing" are available for download at http://www.vestedway.com/vested-library/.
10. Axelrod, 181–185.
11. Roger Fisher and William Ury, *Getting to Yes: Negotiating Agreement Without Giving In* (New York: Houghton Mifflin, 1981). Fisher and Ury advocate for principled negotiation, noting on page xiii of the Introduction that "[t]his book is about the **method** of principled negotiation."
12. Kate Vitasek and Karl Manrodt, with Jeanne Kling, *Vested: How P&G, McDonald's, and Microsoft are Redefining Winning in Business Relationships* (New York: Palgrave Macmillan, 2012).

## 2 TRUST

1. Kenneth Arrow, "Gifts and Exchanges," *Philosophy and Public Affairs* 1 (April 1972): 343–362.
2. "Contract Negotiations Continue to Undermine Value," International Association of Contracting and Commercial Management 2012 Top Terms in Negotiation, April 2013.
3. Adam Smith's *An Inquiry into the Nature of the Wealth of Nations* (1776) is in the public domain and widely available online, such as at http://bartleby.com/10/101.html.
4. Oliver E. Williamson, "Calculativeness, Trust, and Economic Organization," *Journal of Law and Economics* 36, no. 1, part 2, John M. Olin Centennial Conference in Law and Economics at the University of Chicago (Apr. 1993): 453–486.
5. Stephen M. R. Covey, *The Speed of Trust* (New York: Free Press, 2006): 250–253.
6. The Dell-GENCO ATC case study is featured in the second edition of *Vested Outsourcing: Five Rules That Will Transform Outsourcing* by Kate Vitasek with Mike Ledyard and Karl Manrodt (New York: Palgrave Macmillan, 2010). This and all subsequent quotes are taken from the case study.
7. Ibid.
8. Ibid.
9. Ibid.
10. Ibid.
11. Robert Axelrod, *The Evolution of Cooperation* (New York: Houghton Mifflin, 1984): 174.
12. Ibid.
13. Oliver E. Williamson, "Outsourcing: Transaction Cost Economics and Supply Chain Management," *Journal of Supply Chain Management* 44, no. 2 (2008): 5–16.
14. Ibid.
15. Ibid.
16. Ibid.
17. Michael Jackson, "Man in the Mirror," written by Glen Ballard and Siedah Garrett. On the *Bad* album (1988).
18. Interview with Gerald Ledlow and Karl Manrodt, September 2011.

## 3 TRANSPARENCY AND COMPATIBILITY

1. Research interview with confidential source.
2. Research interviews. Subsequent quotes by Hobby and other Sykes personnel taken from the same interviews.
3. J. K. Butler, Jr., "Trust, Expectations, Information Sharing, Climate of Trust, and Negotiation Effectiveness and Effeciency," *Group & Organization Management* 24, no. 2 (1999): 217–38.

4. R. L. Pinkley, "Impact of Knowledge Regarding Alternatives to Settlement in Dyadic Negotiations: Whose Knowledge Counts?" *Journal of Applied Psychology 80* (1995): 403–417.

5. James Tamm and Ronald Luyet, *Radical Collaboration: Five Essential Skills to Overcome Defensiveness and Build Successful Relationships* (New York: HarperCollins, 2004) 105.

6. Ibid.

7. See the Vested Way case study "Vested for Success: How P&G and JLL Transformed Corporate Real Estate," available at http://www.vestedway.com/vested-library/. Subsequent quotes and content come from the study.

8. Tamm and Luyet,105.

9. For more on CaT, see the Vested Website at http://www.vestedway.com/compatibility-and-trust-assessment/.

## 4   STEP 2: CREATING A SHARED VISION

1. Yogi Berra's quote is widely cited. Available at www.rinkworks.com/said/yogiberra.shtml.

2. For a full discussion, see Kate Vitasek and Karl Manrodt, *Vested: How P&G, NcDonald's and Microsoft are Redefining Winning Business Relationships* (New York: Palgrave Macmillan, 2012).

3. Peter Senge, Bryan Smith, Nina Kruschwitz, Joe Lahr, and Sara Schley, *The Necessary Revolution* (New York: Crown Publishing, 2008), 296.

4. Mission statement excerpt from the Water for People website (http://www.waterforpeople.org/).

5. See the Vested Water for People case study, available at http://www.vestedway.com/vested-library/.

6. Water For People Vested case study.

7. Ibid.

8. ARC Advisory Group Brief, "Shared Destiny: Key Lessons from Unipart's Vested Outsourcing Journey with Jaguar and Vodafone," March 2010, 6.

9. Ibid.

10. Ibid.

11. Ibid.

12. J. D. Power press release, available at: www.jdpower.com/autos/articles/2010-Sales-Satisfaction-Index-Study.

13. Research interview with confidential source.

14. Senge, 283.

15. See the Vested Website for information about the Certified Deal Architect Program at http://www.vestedway.com/certified-deal-architect-program/.

16. A Pareto chart, named after Vilfredo Pareto, is a type of chart that contains both bars and a line graph, where individual values are represented in descending order by bars, and the cumulative total is represented by the line.

17. Senge, 295.

## 5 STEP 3: ESTABLISHING THE SIX ESSENTIAL RELATIONSHIP PRINCIPLES

1. See the Vested Way case study "Vested For Success: How P&G and JLL Transformed Corporate Real Estate," available at http://www.vestedway.com/vested-library/. Subsequent quotes from and references to P&G and JLL come from the study.
2. For a discussion of social norms as tools to gain normative leverage in any kind of business negotiation, see David Frydlinger, *Det Affärsjuridiska Hantverket: Arbetet Innanför Avtalsfrihetens Gränser* [The craft of business law: The work within the boundaries of contract freedom), (Stockholm: Norstedts Juridik, 2012).
3. P&G/JLL case study.
4. A Prisoner's Dilemma is a situation, common in society and business, where the short-term self-interest of each party conflicts with the parties' long-term interests. In the long term, they would be better off if they cooperate. In the short term, they would not. See also note 3 in chapter 1.
5. The winner of the tournament was a game called tit-for-tat, using the strategy that starts with cooperation and thereafter does what the other player did on the previous move. As long as the other party cooperated, the party using tit for tat also cooperated. If the other party defected, tit for tat defected. And so on. Tit-for- tat won since it was the strategy that had obtained the greatest rewards when the game was finished. Tit for tat was the strategy that created most value during the game.
6. Mihály Csíkszentmihályi, *The Psychology of Optimal Experience* (New York: Harper & Row, 1990).
7. Malcolm Gladwell, *Outliers: The Story of Success* (New York: Little, Brown, 2008).
8. Daniel H. Pink, *Drive: The Surprising Truth About What Motivates Us* (New York: Riverhead Books, 2009).
9. See the Vested Way case study "Vested For Success: How the Dept. of Energy and CH2M-Hill Transformed a Plutonium Site to Prairie Land," available at http://www.vestedway.com/vested-library/.
10. Research interview with confidential source.
11. Ibid.
12. Dan Ariely is the author of several provocative and entertaining books, including *Predictably Irrational* and *The Upside of Irrationality*. His Website is at http://danariely.com/.
13. Dan Ariely, *The (Honest) Truth About Dishonesty: How We Lie to Everyone—Especially Ourselves* (New York: HarperCollins, 2012).
14. Ibid., 2.
15. Ibid., 3.
16. P&G/JLL Vested case study.
17. Ibid.

18. Mickey Connolly and Richard Rianoshek, *The Communication Catalyst: The Fast (But Not Stupid) Track to Value for Customers, Investors, and Employees.* (Chicago: Dearborn Trade Publishing, 2002), 84
19. Ibid., 85.
20. Ibid., 88.
21. Ibid., 88.
22. Ibid., 88.
23. See the Vested Way case study, "Vested For Success: McDonald's Secret Sauce for Supply Chain Success," available at http://www.vestedway.com/vested-library/.

    Also see Kate Vitasek and Karl Manrodt with Jeanne Kling, *Vested: How P&G, McDonald's, and Microsoft are Redefining Winning in Business Relationships* (New York: Palgrave Macmillan, 2012). Subsequent quotes and content are taken from the book and case study.
24. Vitasek and Manrodt, *Vested*, op cit.
25. Research interview with confidential source.
26. Ibid.
27. Douglass C. North, Nobel Prize lecture, "Economic Performance through Time," December 9, 1993. Available at http://www.nobelprize.org/nobel_prizes/economics/laureates/1993/north-lecture.html.
28. See the discussions of pie-sharing and cooperative exchange norms by Sandy D. Jap, "Pie-Sharing in Complex Collaboration Contexts," *Journal of Marketing Research* (February 2001): 86–99. Also, Janet Bercovitz, Sandy D. Jap, and Jack A. Nickerson, "The Antecedents and Performance Implications of Cooperative Exchange Norms," *Organization Science* 17, no. 6 (November-December 2006): 724–740.
29. OneFinance discussed in Vitasek and Manrodt, *Vested*, op cit.
30. Ibid., chapter 5.
31. Ibid.
32. P&G/JLL case study.
33. Research interview.
34. Based on interviews with confidential sources.

## 6  FOUR RULES

1. Chester L. Karrass, *The Negotiating Game* (New York: HarperBusiness, 1992).
2. Robert Axelrod, *The Evolution of Cooperation* (New York: Basic Books, 1984).
3. Roger Fisher and William Ury, *Getting to Yes: Negotiating Agreement Without Giving In* (New York: Houghton Mifflin, 1981).
4. The following story is based on confidential interviews with persons we call Jack and Sam.
5. Jane Mansbridge, "Taking Coercion Seriously," *Constellations* 3, no. 3 (January 1997): 407–416.

6. As described in chapter 5 of *Vested: How P&G, McDonald's, and Microsoft are Redefining Winning in Business Relationships* by Kate Vitasek and Karl Manrodt with Jeanne Kling (New York: Palgrave Macmillan, 2012).

7. *The Vested Outsourcing Manual: A Guide to Creating Successful Business and Outsourcing Agreements* provides step-by-step guidance to craft the flexible framework that is the contract between two companies. This is especially true for companies seeking to fully embrace and implement Vested's Five Rules.

   Kate Vitasek with Jacqui Crawford, Jeanette Nyden, and Katherine Kawamoto, *The Vested Outsourcing Manual: A Guide to Creating Successful Business and Outsourcing Agreements* (New York: Palgrave Macmillan, 2011).

8. Research interview.

9. See the Vested Way website at http://www.vestedway.com/certified-deal-architect-program/.

10. See the Vested case study, "Vested For Success: How the Dept. of Energy and CH2M-Hill Transformed a Plutonium Site to Prairie Land," available for download at http://www.vestedway.com/vested-library/.

11. Also see chapter 4 of *Vested: How P&G, McDonald's, and Microsoft are Redefining Winning in Business Relationships* by Kate Vitasek and Karl Manrodt with Jeanne Kling (New York: Palgrave Macmillan, 2012).

12. Ibid.

13. Ibid., 69

14. Ibid.

## 7  WIIFWE STYLES, STRATEGIES, AND TACTICS

1. The executive's identity is confidential.

2. Oliver E. Williamson, "Outsourcing: Transaction Cost Economics and Supply Chain Management," *Journal of Supply Chain Management* 44, no. 2 (2008): 10.

3. Ibid.

4. Robert Axelrod, *The Evolution of Cooperation* (New York: Basic Books, 1984).

5. Williamson, "Outsourcing," 10.

6. Marshall L. Fisher, "What is the Right Supply Chain for Your Product?" *Harvard Business Review* (March–April 1997). Reprint available at http://www.computingscience.nl/docs/vakken/ebu/2011/downloads/Fisher.pdf.

7. R. L. Pinkley, "Impact of Knowledge Regarding Alternatives to Settlement in Dyadic Negotiations: Whose Knowledge Counts?" *Journal of Applied Psychology 80* (1995): 403–417.

8. Dan Ariely, *The (Honest) Truth About Dishonesty: How We Lie to Everyone—Especially Ourselves* (New York: HarperCollins, 2012).

9. Williamson, "Outsourcing."

10. Research interview.

11. Tim Venable, "William Reeves: Driving Leading-Edge Service Delivery," *Corporate Real Eastate Leader,* (2005): 60–65.

## 8   NEGOTIATING MONEY FOR MUTUAL BENEFIT

1.  For a thorough explanation on developing pricing models for complex relationships, *The Vested Outsourcing Manual* is a great resource, particularly chapter 6. Kate Vitasek with Jacqui Crawford, Jeanette Nyden, and Katherine Kawamoto, *The Vested Outsourcing Manual: A Guide to Creating Successful Business and Outsourcing Agreements* (New York: Palgrave Macmillan, 2011).

2.  Roger Fisher and William Ury, *Getting to Yes: Negotiating Agreement Without Giving In* (New York: Houghton Mifflin, 1981).

3.  Roy Lewicki, David Saunders, and Bruce Barry, *Negotiation*, 5th ed. (New York: McGraw Hill, 2005).

4.  Ibid., 76

5.  Ibid.

6.  Marcel Mauss, *The Gift* (London and New York:, Routledge 1990), 16f.

7.  For a complete discussion see chapter 4 of *Vested: How P&G, McDonald's, and Microsoft are Redefining Winning in Business Relationships* by Kate Vitasek and Karl Manrodt, with Jeanne Kling (New York: Palgrave Macmillan, 2012).

8.  For a more thorough analysis of the Rocky Flats Closure Project pricing model see *Vested*, p. 73–84.

9.  GAO report to Congress, "Nuclear Cleanup of Rocky Flats: DOE Can Use Lessons Learned to Improve Oversight of Other Sites' Cleanup Activities," July 2006, http://www.gao.gov/products/GAO-06–352.

10. Kaiser-Hill operated under two innovative DOE contracting models at Rocky Flats. The first, awarded in 1995, was the first performance-based contract in DOE. It paid the contractor only for specific units of verifiable work. The model was in sharp contrast to the Maintenance & Operations (M&O) contracts of the day where a contractor's fee was based on subjective performance criteria. Source: http://www.ch2m.com/corporate/services/decontamination_and_decommissioning/assets/ProjectPortfolio/rocky.pdf.

11. See the Vested Way case study "Vested For Success: How the Dept. of Energy and CH2M-Hill Transformed a Plutonium Site to Prairie Land," available at http://www.vestedway.com/vested-library/.

12. Special news broadcast recorded from ABC Evening News for Tuesday, Dec. 20, 1994. Video available from the Vanderbilt Television News Archive at http://tvnews.vanderbilt.edu/siteindex/1994-Specials/special-1994–12–20-ABC-1.html.

13. GAO Report to Congress, op cit.

14. Ibid.

15. K. Cameron and M. Lavine, *Making The Impossible Possible: Leading Extraordinary Performance, The Rocky Flats Story* (San Francisco: Berritt-Koehler, 2006).

## 9   STEP 5: RELATIONSHIP MANAGEMENT

1.  Kate Vitasek with Jacqui Crawford, Jeanette Nyden, and Katherine Kawamoto, *The Vested Outsourcing Manual: A Guide to Creating Successful Business and Outsourcing Agreements* (New York: Palgrave Macmillan, 2011).

2. For a more thorough discussion on how to create a fully Vested governance structure and a detailed explanation of the four elements of a governance structure, refer to *The Vested Outsourcing Manual*, chapter 7.
3. Research interview.
4. The city manager story is based on research interviews.
5. Measurement minutiae is the ninth ailment that can plague outsourcing companies. The hallmark of this ailment is trying to measure everything to get a clear picture of the business processes and functions being outsourced. See Kate Vitasek with Mike Ledyard and Karl Manrodt, *Vested Outsourcing: Five Rules That Will Transform Outsourcing* (New York: Palgrave Macmillan, 2010).
6. Donella Meadows, *Thinking in Systems* (White River Junction, Vt.: Chelsea Green Publishing, 2008).
7. See chapter 5 of *Vested: How P&G, McDonald's, and Microsoft are Redefining Winning in Business Relationships* by Kate Vitasek and Karl Manrodt with Jeanne Kling (New York: Palgrave Macmillan, 2012).
8. See the Vested Way Water for People case study, available at http://www.vestedway.com/vested-library/.
9. Research interview.
10. Research interview.

## 10  THE POWER OF WE

1. The US telecom company and its facilities management service provider story is based on research and interviews with company officials on December 20, 2012. They requested anonymity. All quotes in this section are taken from the interviews.
2. Measurement minutiae is one of the ten ailments that can plague outsourcing companies. See Kate Vitasek with Mike Ledyard and Karl Manrodt, *Vested Outsourcing: Five Rules That Will Transform Outsourcing* (New York: Palgrave Macmillan, 2010).
3. The Reliance CM story is based on research and interviews with company officials on December 12, 2012.
4. Kate Vitasek with Mike Ledyard and Karl Manrodt, *Vested Outsourcing: Five Rules That Will Transform Outsourcing* (New York: Palgrave Macmillan, 2010).

## CONCLUSION

1. Roger Fisher and William Ury, *Getting to Yes: Negotiating Agreement Without Giving In* (New York: Houghton Mifflin, 1981).

# INDEX

Printed in the United States of America